ALLEN
HISTORY
ROANOKE
ESHELMAN
05

ROANOKE

The Renaissance of a Hoosier Village

ROANOKE

The Renaissance of a Hoosier Village

★

Written by

PETE ESHELMAN

and

SCOTT M. BUSHNELL

★

PHOTOGRAPHY RESEARCH BY

PAMELA T. GRAY

GUILD PRESS
EMMIS BOOKS

GUILD PRESS EMMIS BOOKS
40 Monument Circle
Indianapolis, Indiana 46204

ISBN 1-57860-137-1
Library of Congress Control Number 2003106835

Frontespiece: Roanoke's Main Street in the late nineteenth century by Bob Rose

Interior and text design by Sheila G. Samson

Dust jacket design by Listenberger Design Associates

Front dust jacket art: *Spirit of Roanoke* by David J. Gray

To all of us temporary residents on this planet, who dedicate their lives to making the world a better place — in our own backyard.

— Pete & Scott

Contents

Small-town America — America's Jewels

At one time in our country's history, small towns were the American way of life. Villages were carved out of the wilderness principally because of necessity: the providing of safe harbors and trading facilities at the convergence of waterways or at a crossroads serving fertile lands. In other cases, towns came into existence because of man-made opportunities, such as the availability of a lock on a great canal.

As a country, our values today are imbedded in the lessons we learned as a country of small towns—values such as self-reliance, honesty, hard work, commitment to family, education, freedom to live amid diversity of spiritual choices, humility, and willingness to band together and sacrifice when those qualities were needed in times of hardship. Small towns were places in which your neighbors helped you and you helped them. Streets were safe and community pride contributed to a high quality of life. People knew each other and each person meant something.

Small town values are not merely nostalgic memories, but ways of functioning in society: fundamental necessities to the American way of life in the twenty-first century. Yet, by the 1960s, the very survival of many small towns across America was at risk. The migration to cities had taken its toll on village populations. Interstate highways bypassed many small towns, devastating downtown commercial centers. Mass marketing changed consumer buying habits at the expense of local merchants.

By the 1980s, many small towns had gone off the map and become footnotes in history. Other small towns tried to hold on to the "good ol' days" even though their economy, tax base and young people had abandoned them. Many towns that struggled to stay alive showed the strain with boarded-up buildings, dilapidated streets and sidewalks, inadequately maintained sewer and water infrastructures and declining populations. By the 1990s, most small towns bypassed by interstate highways in rural America were either dying or gone.

Roanoke is a small town located in northeast Indiana, and its evolution is typical of that of small-town America. Founded on the site of Indian hunting grounds, it was established as a settlement to serve the needs of workmen and passengers on a lock on the Wabash & Erie Canal. During its history Roanoke grew and prospered, but by the 1980s its painful decline was evident.

What makes Roanoke unique is that this small northeastern Indiana town stepped away from the brink of extinction and managed to nurture itself back to stability and prosperity. In 2003, it is recognized as the "crown jewel" in its county and can serve as an example for other small towns in America which are seeking revival.

What caused Roanoke's renaissance? The spark began in 1990 when a new company moved to town. As that company grew into an American success story, so did its commitment to Roanoke. This is the story of how one small town revived, how one business sparked its restoration, and how precious small town values can be used as the catalyst for revival.

— Pete Eshelman, President and CEO, American Specialty

INTRODUCTION

I HAVE not met a person anywhere in the world who did not desire "Life, Liberty, and the Pursuit of Happiness." Our founding fathers were right on. Unfortunately, in today's world most people don't have this opportunity. Fortunately, we as Americans do.

I was taught these values growing up in my family. I am a member of the Baby Boomer generation and saw my parents striving to build a new life in post-World War II America. My mom and dad worked hard, Dad to make money in pursuit of the American dream for his family and Mom at home raising three children. My parents taught me strong values, gave me a solid education, taught me to be a good person, and most important, they believed in me. I am fortunate to have great parents whom I love and admire. I was inspired by their example to fulfill the American dream.

Sports became my first opportunity to test my character, and as an athlete I learned what it took to be successful. My dad had taught me that success required hard work, persistence, preparation, and knowing your business better than anyone else. His favorite saying was, "Success is luck. The harder you work, the luckier you get!"

To make money during the off-season before the New York Yankees' minor league spring training, I worked as a chauffeur in Miami. My employer was a man from Wabash, Indiana, who invented the Yellow Pages. L. M. Berry had a true "rags to riches" Horatio Alger story. He was a mentor to my father and gave to me, in effect, a graduate school education. As I drove him about, I asked him questions about his business life. He taught me about the value of focus, use of time, always seeing the big picture, and treating everyone with respect.

When a shoulder injury ended my career as a baseball player, I went to work for the New York Yankees at Yankee Stadium, working for the man who changed the professional sports industry from a fledgling business into a multibillion-dollar industry. George Steinbrenner taught me about the "will to win" in a big league world. As I ended my sports career, I entered the insurance business in Boston selling life insurance and learned the tough lessons of starting a business from scratch. But I also found great satisfaction in helping people help themselves. I learned self-reliance and the meaning behind the saying, "the only security in life is the security you create for yourself."

I started a sports insurance business with partners and then sold my interest. I learned the lessons it had to teach, joined a large company, enjoyed the challenge, but longed to be an entrepreneur again.

In 1989, in the basement of my house, my brother, Tim, a friend and business associate, Dave Harris, and I started American Specialty, a company dedicated to providing specialized insurance for the sports and entertainment industry. We had a great business idea and hit it at the right time: the beginning of the golden era of the sports and entertainment industry.

In 1990 we moved to Roanoke with three employees. At the time, we had no idea how important this decision would be for the development of our company and our influence on Roanoke. Today, fourteen years later, our business has grown to become the industry leader, and our facilities have expanded from one building in Roanoke to twenty buildings and parcels of land in downtown Roanoke, our Corporate Campus.

I have been asked many times about our company's influence on the revival of Roanoke, which many people have called "Roanoke's renaissance." My response is straightforward: "Our corporate life and the renaissance of Roanoke are inextricably intertwined."

This book has been written to tell that story and written especially for:

- Those who live and work in Roanoke and other small towns across America which are struggling and seeking revival.

- Our clients who have enabled us to build the company we dreamed of, a company with a "heart."

- Our employees who have provided the "hearts."

- Anyone with a "heart" who wants to make a difference in his or her own backyard.

— Pete Eshelman

"There is no limit to the good a man can do if he doesn't care who gets the credit."

CHAPTER 1

ROANOKE'S FIRST INHABITANTS

Our system is to live in perpetual peace with the Indians, to cultivate an affectionate attachment from them, by everything just and liberal which we can do for them within the bounds of reason, and by giving them effectual protection against wrongs of our own people. The decrease of game rendering their subsistence by hunting insufficient, we wish to draw them to agriculture, to spinning and weaving. . . . Our settlements will gradually circumscribe and approach the Indians, and they will in time either incorporate with us as citizens of the United States, or remove beyond the Mississippi. The former is certainly the termination of their history more happy for themselves; but, in the whole course of this, it is essential to cultivate their love. As to their fear, we presume that our strength and their weakness is now so visible that they must see we have only to shut our hand to crush them, and that all our liberalities to them proceed from motives of pure humanity only.

— Thomas Jefferson, in a letter to
Governor William H. Harrison, February 27, 1803

THE EARLIEST history of Roanoke begins with the small, shallow stream that flows east of the town. Though it is difficult to imagine today, the Little Wabash, or the Little River as it is more commonly known, was part of the strategically important development of northeastern Indiana and northwestern Ohio. The Little River once wound through a twenty-five-thousand-acre marshland teeming with wildlife. In some areas it traversed soggy grassland; in others it was a wide stream. Either way, it was a well-known portion of a major route for native Americans, trappers, and pioneers that ultimately linked the Great Lakes to the Gulf of Mexico.

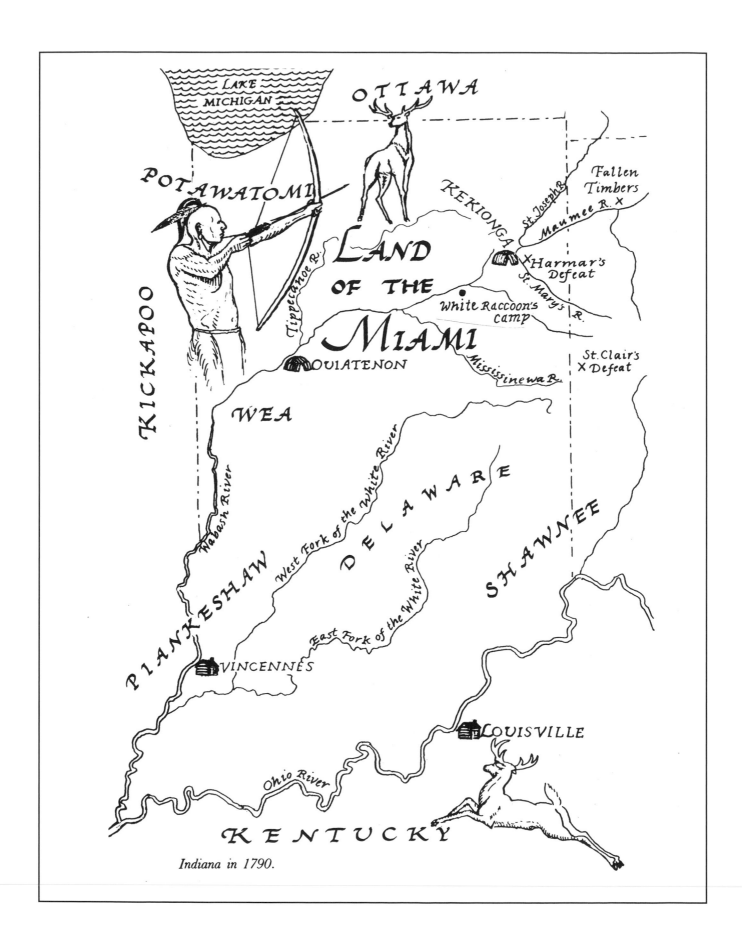

LAKE MICHIGAN

OTTAWA

POTAWATOMI

KICKAPOO

Fallen Timbers

KEKIONGA

St. Joseph R.

Maumee R. X

Tippecanoe R.

Land of the Miami

X Harmar's Defeat

St. Mary's R.

White Raccoon's camp

OUIATENON

Mississinewa R.

St. Clair's X Defeat

WEA

Wabash River

West Fork of the White River

DELAWARE

SHAWNEE

PIANKESHAW

East Fork of the White River

VINCENNES

LOUISVILLE

Ohio River

KENTUCKY

Indiana in 1790.

Early hunters could travel up the Maumee to the St. Mary's River south of what is now Fort Wayne and then carry their canoes over an easily accessible, nine-mile portage to the Little River. From there, they would be able to reach the Wabash, then the Ohio and the Mississippi rivers before arriving at the Gulf of Mexico. The existence of the portage and the Little River shaped the future of this country by helping to open its rich land to exploration, hunting, settlement and agriculture. For two hundred years, Native Americans, French and British fur traders, as well as immigrant settlers, all used this route for exploration and for commerce.

The portage may have been used for centuries before European settlement began in North America, but it is only historically traceable to the Miami Indians who resided south of the Great Lakes in the late 1600s.

The first recorded contact with the Miami by the French explorers of North America came not in northeastern Indiana, but in eastern Wisconsin in 1654. The Miami had been driven there by the Iroquois sometime before 1640. The Miami were a great nation, and a French trapper estimated their number at more than twenty thousand near the Fox River in Wisconsin. This was likely an exaggeration. Where these Algonquian-language people lived prior to that is open to speculation, but it is believed they had been driven westward and northward by the Iroquois.

The Miami prospered at farming most of the year, and were hunter-gatherers in the winter. They were also accomplished traders, establishing major villages along rivers and portages between major rivers. As a result, the Miami came into contact with many cultures and were able to incorporate elements of these cultures into their lives. For example, the Miami grew a soft yellow corn more commonly found among western tribes, rather than the flint corn grown by eastern tribes. Their adaptability helped the Miami to trade with both the French and the English at a time when the two European nations were struggling for domination of North America.

When the Miami migrated to southern Michigan and northern Indiana and then to the upper Wabash Valley in the 1670s, they were fewer in number than recorded two decades earlier. Like many Native American tribes, the Miami had been devastated by epidemics of European diseases. Still, the missionaries of the time identified six Miami-speaking groups, three of which became tribes: the Wea, the Piankashaw and the Atchatchakangouen. The last named was also known as the Crane Band Miami, which settled where the St. Joseph and St. Mary's rivers form the Maumee River in what is now Fort Wayne. They called their village Kekionga. According to one legend, the word meant "blackberry patch." Another Miami interpretation was that the name indicated the most ancient Miami village in the region. Some of their tribe formed villages just beyond the portage, near what is now Roanoke. As a tribe, the Miami claimed dominion over all of Indiana and western Ohio. This was not to last forever.

A factor in the Miami development in northeastern Indiana was the geography of the area which provided some security. The Miami were able to recover from recurrent epidemics and remain somewhat aloof from the war because the Great Black Swamp—an expanse of almost impassable wetlands and woodlands stretching from what is now Fort Wayne to Findlay, Ohio—formed a natural barrier between them and the mass of settlers. The dense canopy of oaks combined with the marshland to harbor a rich diversity of wildlife, the most formidable of which may have been disease-carrying mosquitoes and other water-borne illnesses. Apparently able to cope with the swampy terrain, the Miami were able to prosper at Kekionga—as the principal village at the junction of the three rivers was known—and in a smaller village which was closer to Roanoke near the Little River for almost ninety years. Two other smaller villages were on the Elkhart River and at the mouth of the Eel River near present-day Logansport. Contemporary estimates put the entire Miami population at about one thousand in 1778. While this number may seem small, the tribe was able to survive and even thrive because of its location and its trade practices.

While a great deal of history has been recorded about Kekionga, there has been little written about the smaller Miami village sometimes recorded on maps as Raccoon's Village and on others as White Raccoon's Village along the Little River near Roanoke. There undoubtedly was commerce between this village and Kekionga, as well as with passing trappers and traders.

In February 1823, Henry Hay wrote that White Raccoon's village was located "twelve miles from Fort Wayne." The former Indian agent said the inhabitants had two log houses and some hogs and cattle.

Despite the swampy conditions along the Little River, it is evident that the Miami used the waterway for transportation. There also was ample evidence of Miami campgrounds in the Roanoke area as late as the start of the twentieth century. Many older residents tell of finding arrowheads and broken items in fields. One very rich source of arrow and spearheads was the area now at the corner of South Main and Vine streets where Miami apparently had camped with some regularity.

Their relatively peaceful life was soon to end. Between 1760 and 1794 the frontier in northern Indiana was torn by almost constant warfare between the Miami (and sometimes their confederates) and the expanding powers of a developing nation. Warrior chiefs like Little Turtle led the Miami and their allies, sometimes brilliantly, against the Europeans who wished to occupy Indian lands.

After the eighteenth-century wars between the Miami and the new American nation ended in victory over the Indians, the question of distribution of lands came to the forefront. General Anthony Wayne crafted the Treaty of Greenville in 1795 that set the pattern for the more than three hundred treaties that were to follow in the next eighty years with various tribes. It repudiated earlier treaties, set a boundary for Indian country, granted Indians hunting rights and promised that the U.S. government would care for them. It also contained the requirement that if the Indians were to ever sell their land, it would have to be sold to the U.S. government. This set the stage for the Indian cessions of the nineteenth century and thereby for villages like Roanoke to come into being.

Little Turtle went on to become an influential "peace chief" until his death in 1812. In the years between 1803 and 1809, the Miami ceded the southern third of Indiana to the U.S. government. The leadership of the Miami fell to Jean Baptiste Richardville—a nephew of Pacanne, a prominent Miami chief from the 1750s to about 1815, and son of a French trader—who was adept at commerce in both the French and Miami worlds. His skills were particularly important as the Indian nations were forced to leave Indiana.

In 1818 the Miami ceded all of central Indiana with the exception of "the Miami National Reserve" and then all of the land north of the Wabash in 1826. In 1830, Congress passed the Indian Removal Act, and by 1840 all of the Miami land—with the exception of few tracts—were ceded. White Raccoon's Village disappeared from the maps of the Roanoke area. Removal of all but one hundred members of the Miami tribe to the Kansas Territory occurred in 1846. Twenty-seven years later, the Miami who had moved to Kansas sold their land in that state and were relocated on a reservation in northeastern Oklahoma.

The name of Jean Baptiste Richardville is well known in the Roanoke area, as it is throughout northern Indiana. Throughout the Miami's final period in Indiana, Richardville was the primary intermediary between the American government and the tribe. This leader was acutely aware of the pressure of settlers on the U.S. government. At the same time, he knew that the Miami were painfully aware of other removals, notably the Potawatomi deportation in 1836, in which the Indians were forced to walk under military guard and suffered greatly from disease and malnutrition. It also was obvious that the tide of settlement was overwhelming. Northern Indiana underwent significant growth in the 1830s as the population north of the Wabash River rose from 3,380 in 1830 to 65,897 in 1840. In the same period, the Miami and Potawatomi declined from 5,000 to 800.

Richardville, through personal appeals to Congress and through court rulings, helped delay the removal of the Miami until 1846 to allow tribal members to liquidate other landholdings and sell goods before the journey west. In 1872 the Commission on Indian Affairs submitted a bill to Congress recognizing the Indians as individuals. No longer would tribes be recognized as negotiating bodies. Richardville, who died in

Chief Little Turtle

1841, had foreseen the future for his people: He had arranged for unallotted lands in the Roanoke area to be sold, with all revenues placed in individual annuity accounts.

The families of Richardville and others were allowed to remain in the area through individual treaties. One Miami who remained in the Roanoke area was an aged woman named Kilsoquah. The granddaughter of Chief Little Turtle and the widow of Antoine Revarre, or White Loon, Kilsoquah was the focus of great attention. She lived with her son, Anthony, or Tony Loon, as he was called by town residents, smoking her corncob pipe and speaking only the Miami language.

In 1910 thousands of people gathered in Roanoke to pay her homage as "the last of the Miami tribe." She was not the last by any means since there were other full Miami in Grant and Miami counties as well as at least one other in Huntington County and, of course, many in Oklahoma. That, however, didn't stop the romantics of the era. Under the leadership of the Improved Order of Red Men (who espoused patriotic ideals fostered, they said, by the Boston Tea Party in which colonists dressed as Indians dumped British-taxed tea into Boston harbor), religious services, speeches and a parade were held in Roanoke for Kilsoquah. She rode in an automobile provided by E. E. Richards, while Tony Loon rode in another late model car provided by the Zent family. The newspapers estimated the crowd at ten thousand, which, if it is an accurate number, was a prodigious number of people for the town at the time. The 1910 census showed that Roanoke's population was a little over five hundred.

After refusing to go to Kansas with the rest of the Miami, Kilsoquah and her son lived east of the town in what became known as Indian Hill. But Kilsoquah's daughter, Mary, went with the tribe, was educated in government schools, and became a teacher. Neither mother nor daughter communicated with each other, and it was not until 1912 that they discovered the other party was still alive. Kilsoquah, Tony, and Mary reunited during the daughter's brief visit to Roanoke in 1913.

Kilsoquah died in September 1915. Miami Indian census rolls indicate her age

Jean Baptiste Richardville

was eighty-five at the time, but her grave marker states that she was 105. Her son, Tony Loon, died in 1918 and was buried next to his mother on a knoll in Glenwood Cemetery.

Tony's passing brought to a close the daily reminders of Roanoke's origins in the time before European settlement. The region had gone from being barely inhabited by Indians to a commercial center on the Wabash & Erie Canal in about a century. There were even greater changes to come in the next one hundred years.

Kilsoquah, whose name reportedly meant "Setting Sun," and her son , Anthony Revarre, known as Tony Loon, were honored in Roanoke in 1910.

The Miami at War

The confrontation of Native Americans and Europeans in northeastern Indiana occurred in three phases—the French, British, and American—over about 150 years. The French were the first to recognize the potential of the region, engaging in trapping and trading with the Miami and other tribes for furs. The Miami also found that they benefited from trading with the British. Eventually, however, the European wars between the British and the French spilled over into North America and the Miami became part of what was a protracted conflict. The Miami proved themselves to be great warriors, often led by exceptional chiefs. Following are some of the major events of the conflict:

- The Miami were allies of the French in their defeat of English General Edward Braddock in western Pennsylvania in 1755. Among the officers serving with Braddock was a young colonial, Major George Washington. Believed to be among the Miami was a young warrior named Little Turtle.

- In 1780 a small French military force traveled up the Wabash and Little rivers and plundered the Miami village at Kekionga before retreating to an area on Aboite Creek, about four miles east of Roanoke. Little Turtle and his warriors surprised the French and massacred them.

- The Miami resisted the growing pressure of white settlers, particularly after the passage of the Northwest Ordinance in 1787 which established how new states would be created from Indian lands. As a result of the Miami resistance, the period from 1790 to 1794 was known as Little Turtle's War.

- In the fall of 1790, President George Washington sent Josiah Harmar, a Revolutionary War soldier, to punish the Miami and their allies for their incursions. Harmar and his men arrived at Kekionga on October 17 and found the village deserted. They destroyed 180 log houses and 20,000 bushels of corn. Overconfident, Harmar sent some of his troops back to Cincinnati and waited with the rest to ambush the Miami when they returned to Kekionga. Instead, Little Turtle surprised Harmar's army and killed 183 Americans.

- Washington then ordered Major General Arthur St. Clair to assemble an army in the following year. Washington, from his personal experience with the Miami, personally warned the general to be wary of a surprise attack by the Miami. The warning fell on deaf ears. The march to Kekionga was difficult for St. Clair's army, with supply problems, desertions, unruly Kentucky militia and an ungainly group of camp followers accompanying the troops. There was little if any inkling among the Americans that Little Turtle wanted revenge for the destruction of Kekionga and had assembled more than a thousand warriors from traditional allies of the Miami. Just before dawn on November 4, 1791, the Indians surprised St. Clair's army southeast of Fort Wayne and routed the Americans in a grisly battle. Official sources listed 630 officers and enlisted men killed. There may have been another 100 women and children camp followers also slain. It was the single largest defeat by a U.S. army at the hands of native Americans.

- In 1794, General Anthony Wayne led the third and largest campaign against the Miami. Wayne succeeded by carefully training and equipping his army. He marched through Ohio, building forts, guarding his supply lines and making peace overtures to tribes formerly allied with the Miami. Interestingly, Little Turtle counseled the Miami to negotiate peace with Wayne, but to no avail. In the summer of 1794, Wayne first defeated the Indians at the Battle of Fort Recovery and then again in August at the Battle of Fallen Timbers near Toledo. He marched on Kekionga along the northern bank of the Maumee River and built a fort that bore his name.

CHAPTER 2

THE GREAT CANAL

The condition of the country from Fort Wayne to Roanoke was so incredibly stamped on my youthful mind that it can never be erased. The beautiful farms, fields and homes that you now behold as you travel along the Little River Valley was then a dismal swamp, consisting of black mire, stagnant water, old logs, trees, mosquitoes, snakes, frogs and ague germs.

I doubt if the swamps of the Nile can produce a more God-forsaken and desolate stretch than was the Little River Valley, now scarcely more than a creek, in those days and yet, it would seem that in the creation it was designed that even this most despised portion of Indiana should donate their share of sustenance to the hardy race of pioneers. For here, wild geese, ducks and other water fowl swarmed in innumerable flocks, the river swarmed with fish, however.

— Frank Sumner Bash recalling his arrival in the 1850s

THE THREAT of conflict with the Indians was gone and northern Indiana found itself part of a great Midwestern migration that sent thousands of settlers into states like Indiana, Michigan, Wisconsin, and Illinois. All over mid-America an agrarian population was clamoring for better ways to open the country and to move their products to market. Towns sprang up every ten miles or so, since that was the limit a horse-drawn wagon could travel in a day to buy supplies and sell goods. There was a growing need for easier means for long-distance commerce. After considerable debate, Congress provided financing for internal improvements and state governments eagerly incurred indebtedness to build canals, better roads and eventually railroads.

The Wabash & Erie Canal was symbolic of the great expectations that the rapidly expanding young nation harbored in the early 1800s. The success of the Erie Canal in western New York precipitated similar projects in several states—particularly Ohio and Pennsylvania—that were made profitable by the "Great Migration" of settlers. Indiana was soon to follow.

Canals were costly to build, and the work required for the Indiana section of the Wabash & Erie Canal, whose route went through Roanoke, illustrates that fact. Begun in 1832, the canal route required a sixty-four-foot-wide forest path to be "grubbed out," with trees and brush removed within twenty feet of either side. Horse- or mule-drawn scoops dredged out the worst, but the manpower —primarily Irish immigrants who received ten dollars a month plus food and rations of whiskey—really dug the canal. Accidents and disease were very common and victims were buried along the route in large numbers. Malaria, cholera and other diseases claimed the lives of so many workers that salaries were raised to sixteen to twenty dollars a month, while whiskey rations were increased, too, to attract new workers.

Water finally poured into "the long ditch" and the section of the canal from Fort Wayne to Huntington was opened July 4, 1835, with a series of celebrations, including one in Roanoke. History books report that Asa Fairfield piloted the canal boat *Indiana* along the route, but there is little recorded of what was said at each stop. The gathering at Roanoke may have been small, since the area was still sparsely populated.

It would take eight more years before the canal was operational from Lake Erie to Lafayette, a distance of about 250 miles that could be traversed in fifty-six hours in a boat pulled by four to six mules walking along a towpath. The canal eventually reached Evansville and the Ohio River in 1853, becoming the longest canal in the Western Hemisphere—468 miles.

Navigation was not always easy. The shallow waters froze during the winter months, and transportation was often halted during spring thaws that caused breaches in the canal, when water would pour out onto the farmlands. A minimum of four feet

Roanoke in the nineteenth century.

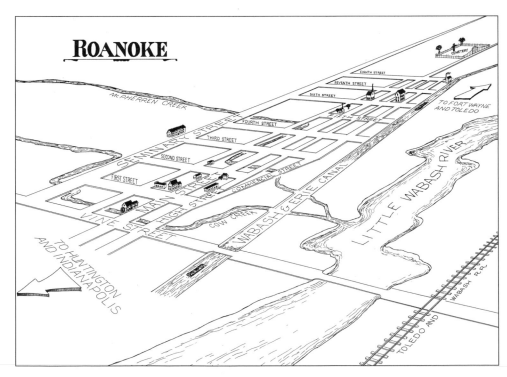

of water was necessary for navigation, and the system required constant maintenance and dredging to keep the boats operating. Then there were the freakish acts of nature. A disastrous flood in 1836, for example, stranded some vessels for two weeks as debris choked the channel and breached the canal. Most of the breaches occurred south of Roanoke, stranding travelers and workers in the town for days at a time.

The physical problems of the canal were not the most serious problem, though, and the system's demise could be foreseen even in its heyday. It proved consistently unprofitable. The canals were the nation's earliest internal improvement projects. The land for the Wabash & Erie Canal in Indiana, for example, was owned by the federal government as a result of 1826 treaties with the Potawatomi and Miami Indians. It was ceded to the state, which financed the construction through the sale of bonds. The nation's financial crises of 1837 to 1843 helped devalue the state bonds, and the tolls paid by shippers and travelers never covered operating expenses. As a result, the state was unable to even make interest payments to bondholders.

In 1847 Indiana's governor asserted that the state would not renege on its bond as some other states had; however, the bondholders were unsatisfied and convinced the legislature to surrender the canal and one million acres of unsold land. In return, a private management team promised to complete the canal to Evansville if the state would assume the remaining portion of the debt and interest. This arrangement proved to be a poor deal for both sides. Indiana's reputation as a government entity worthy of investment was damaged, and the private management group lost about $2.5 million in its twenty-seven years of running the canal.

Still, the impact of the Wabash & Erie Canal was profound for northern Indiana. The economic impact can be clearly seen in the number of bushels of corn shipped out of Toledo, which originated in the Maumee and Wabash valleys. In 1844 the total was 5,262 bushels; in 1846, 555,250 bushels; and 2,775,149 bushels in 1851.

Towns like Roanoke that serviced canal boats and built mills and warehouses along the canal were direct beneficiaries in other ways, too. Some immigrant workers who came to build the canal settled in the community. Merchants who arrived to trade with canal workers and passengers often decided that Roanoke was a good destination, sparking innovation and creativity. For example, the first steam-powered canal boats were built in Roanoke and fitted for engines in Fort Wayne. Newspapers record that the first steam-powered boat passed through Roanoke on the canal in September 1852.

The architecture of downtown Roanoke is a visible reminder of the town's prosperous times, though no mercantile buildings remain from the canal era. The streets are still set on the grid around the canal, flowing north on the east side of the village. The commercial success of the town also persisted. A young pioneer village along the Wabash & Erie Canal at its inception, the community's downtown area maintained its stature as a center of commerce through most of the whirlwind changes of the nineteenth and twentieth centuries. As newer forms of transportation opened the nation to commerce and travel, Roanoke was resilient. Whether it was the railroad replacing the canal or the automobile replacing the horse and buggy, there were citizens eager to adapt to and capitalize on the change. In doing so, they helped the town to grow. It was very much a story of the development of the modern United States from the mid-1800s.

It was not until 1889 that the Little River and most of its tributaries were dredged and the swampland drained. One of the most important branch ditches was one that redirected water from Aboite Creek into Little River. Another part of the project channeled Cow Creek in Roanoke into the river. The fifty-mile dredging project reclaimed an estimated thirty-five thousand acres of land, replacing swampy marshes with fields of corn, oats or wheat as well as pastureland.

By the 1850s when the young Frank Sumner Bash arrived in the community with his family, farming was taking hold and the canal was in its second decade of operation. In Roanoke, Main Street ran down the hill from Eighth Street along a well-platted town. The earliest photographs show a well-worn way with some homes and barns occupying some of the original forty lots registered by a land speculator named George Chapman.

The significance of the role of transportation in the history of Roanoke cannot be overstated. The reason for the development of the community—and indirectly the demise of the swamp that inhibited any earlier settlement—was the canal, just to the east of what is now Main Street. Main Street wasn't the main street at the time. In fact, it paled in comparison to Commercial Street where stores, warehouses and stables served the canal traffic as the town came into being.

Jared Darrow is credited with clearing land and building one of the first homes in Roanoke in 1837, and his family was followed a year later by the Decker family, K. L. Eskridge and Frank Dupuy. Yet, though the cultivation of the land soon became important, it was not farming that ensured the future of the town; rather, it was the

Keeping the Little River clear was a continual effort after the 1889 drainage project was complete. In 1918, this crane on a steam-powered floating dredge worked on the river about a half-mile north of Roanoke.

happenstance of geography that made Roanoke an important place along the canal. It was the ideal location for a lock.

In 1853, when Dr. Sylvanus Koontz arrived via the canal as a boy of nine, there were 150 residents in the village. Although reportedly named Roanoke in 1850 by one of its earliest residents who had lived in the western Virginia community of the same name, the village was better known to the outside world as "The Lock," a reference to the canal's Dickey Lock. The ninety-foot-long and fifteen-foot-wide enclosure raised and lowered the water required to allow a packet or freight boat to traverse the next section of the canal. The lock at Roanoke was sixteen miles from the summit level at Fort Wayne, a distance that represented one of the longest open stretches of the Wabash & Erie Canal. The presence of the lock at Roanoke meant that crews could change the mules pulling the boats and replenish supplies while passengers could disembark to buy food and drink, and perhaps spend the night.

The canal is tightly tied to Roanoke's economic growth. It provided a direct, more accessible route to Fort Wayne, Lake Erie and, eventually, the East Coast. Similarly, when it was completed, the canal was a link to central and southern Indiana, the Ohio River and, eventually, the Mississippi River. Just as the Miami and the *coureurs des bois,* as the French trappers were known, had used this waterway from the Great Lakes to the Mississippi portaging their well-designed canoes, so did the new generation of Americans using its invention—the canal. Packets and barges moved people, animals and goods along the waterway. The smaller packets handled the short-distance runs, while freight barges delivered crops to market and manufactured goods to villages and towns along the canal.

The establishment of a store and a flour mill brought permanence to the Roanoke settlement. These enterprises were followed by restaurants and hotels that served canal workers and travelers, mostly on the town side of the canal. Stables were located on the towpath side. In addition, boat builders, blacksmiths, tack repair shops and warehouses grew up around the lock. William Corkens, for example, became a successful boat builder and proprietor of a boatyard on Commercial Street near Fourth Street, close to the turnaround basin east of the lock.

The first businessman with a sustained record of success in Roanoke was not a miller or a liveryman though, but a druggist. Reuben C. Ebersole operated from a building on the canal, providing a daily dosage of quinine at the lock to those with malaria, or what canal workers then referred to as "the plague." His was a very different business from today's pharmacy. In an 1858 advertisement in the *Huntington Herald,* Ebersole proudly proclaimed: "I would call attention of the world and all the rest of mankind to my assortment of drugs, medicines, alabaster and rouge, rose and bear's oil, wines, liquors and gin for mechanical and chemical purposes." Ebersole eventually moved his drugstore to the corner of North Main and Second streets, where it set the stage for future, more educated pharmacists to serve the town.

As the nineteenth century progressed, Roanoke became an ever more flourishing town. In post-Civil War Roanoke, there were almost thirty commercial operations: three stores selling dry goods; three stores selling boots and shoes; two clothing stores and two milliners; two drugstores; two livery stables; three blacksmiths; one wagon

Reuben C. Ebersole's drugstore was one of the first commercial establishments on the Wabash & Erie Canal in Roanoke. Ebersole was well known for prescribing daily doses of quinine to offset the malaria contracted by canal workers.

Augustus Wasmuth (at far right) was perhaps the most successful pioneer businessman in Roanoke, starting an agricultural implements store, a hardware store, a lumberyard and a bank in a twenty-one-year period in the nineteenth century.

Roanoke's first commercial district in 1870. In the upper left, the square structure with a window is actually a canal boat on the Wabash & Erie Canal. The building in the middle of the row is the drugstore owned by Dr. C. L. Richart (inset, lower right).

William McPherren stands outside Dague's Mill on North Main Street. Flour and grist mills served the farmers throughout the area and helped secure Roanoke's place as an important trading center.

maker; one harness and carriage builder; two sawmills; two saloons; an undertaker; a cigar maker; an attorney; a postmaster; a railroad agent; and a notary public.

Among the early pioneers was Augustus Wasmuth, who rose from indentured servant to prominent businessman and bank founder. The two buildings that serve as the anchors at the northern edge of Roanoke's historic downtown today were built by Wasmuth.

After the Civil War, Roanoke was considered "the best trading and shipping point on the canal between the cities of Fort Wayne and Peru," Indiana, according to the 1887 edition of *The History of Huntington County*. By 1876, when the canal right-of-way was sold off, Roanoke had clinched its reputation as the trading center for the region.

Those days of families traveling by water, mules pulling canal boats, and the raucous laughter of the canal men were gone by the 1880s. Since its demise, the canal has been filled in, paved over, and almost forgotten. To preserve the history of the waterway, the Canal Society of Indiana was formed in 1982 and has championed research into the Wabash & Erie Canal.

The Roanoke Heritage Center dedicated a state historical marker commemorating the location of Dickey Lock at the junction of Second Street and U.S. Highway 24 in August 1997. Dignitaries from the town, county, state legislature and the Canal Society of Indiana marked the occasion with speeches and song. As the master of ceremonies, American Specialty CEO Pete Eshelman paid tribute to the events that defined Roanoke's past and present:

> In today's information age, geography loses its importance as a defining element of history. Distance and physical barriers are spanned by the transfer of data over networks, not by the movement of people and goods over canals, railroads, and highways. One-hundred sixty-two years ago geography dictated the founding of Roanoke with the Wabash & Erie Canal. The canal was replaced by the railroad, which in turn was succeeded by the interurban line, which was later replaced by Highway 24. Today, we have a new highway, the information highway, where businesses and families communicate over networks. But it all started with the canal, and we need to pay tribute to this historic relic and the founding of our town.

In 1999 the Indiana State Historical Society removed timbers from the canal's Culvert 36 in Roanoke for a permanent display in Indianapolis.

Before the advent of interstate highways and easy air travel, transportation went through many metamorphases. As seen in this photo of the J. H. Warner blacksmith shop on North Main Street (right), the rural nature of small-town America meant that the two eras of transportation — horse-drawn and gasoline-powered — sometimes came together in unlikely situations. A blacksmith's shop from the canal era as depicted by Roanoke's Bob Rose (above).

CHAPTER 3

ALWAYS ON A TRAVELED ROAD

THE RAILROAD

Railroad iron is a magician's rod, in its power to evoke the sleeping energies of the land and water. The railroad is but one arrow in our quiver, though it has great value as a sort of yard-stick, and surveyor's line. The bountiful continent is ours, state on state, and territory on territory, to the waves of the Pacific sea.

— Ralph Waldo Emerson, *The Young American*, February 7, 1844

EVEN AT the height of the canal era in Roanoke, the way was being laid for a faster, more efficient and more profitable form of transportation. In 1834, a year before the canal reached Roanoke, the Illinois legislature funded the building of a steam railroad from Quincy on the Mississippi River to the Indiana state line. Four years later the region's first locomotive was hoisted onto an eight-mile section of track at Meredosia, Illinois, to transport a party of VIPs to the end of the line and back again. The route which grew from this modest beginning was called "The Northern Cross" (after an important trail named the "Northern Crossing"), and it would reach Roanoke in less than two decades.

The Northern Cross became the Sangamon and Morgan Railroad and in 1853 the Great Western, at which time the new tracks were laid eastward. In 1856 a new merger created the Toledo, Wabash and Western Railroad, and the main line (being built from both the east and the west) was extended to pass a mile east of downtown Roanoke.

The arrival of the railroad was not as fortuitous for Roanoke as the opening of the canal had been. The competition among existing communities to be located along a railroad route was extreme because of its promise of great prosperity. Proof of the railroad's economic advantages was seen in the growth of Chicago. Once a small outpost on Lake Michigan, the city's population grew 274 percent between 1850 and 1860. Further evidence of the railroads' impact can be found in the 1890 U.S. Census, which put Chicago's population at 1,099,850, or thirty-five times larger than in 1850.

Roanoke was not as fortunate as Chicago was, even though it remained in close proximity to the railroad right-of-way. Roanoke wanted to bring the railroad into the center of town in order to continue its economic growth. Instead, it became engaged in a political battle with the folks in nearby Mahon, a battle marked by political intrigue and a surprising outcome.

These railroad feuds among towns were surprisingly common. At stake here was the opportunity to be located along one leg of a great "iron triangle" connecting Toledo, Decatur, Illinois, and Chicago. Traveling southwest from Toledo on the Decatur line, trains rolled through Defiance, Ohio; Woodburn, Fort Wayne, Roanoke, Huntington, Peru, and Logansport to Attica, Indiana; and Danville, Illinois. The potential economic benefits of railroad access on this line were obvious to businessmen in Roanoke and Mahon.

Like its neighbor to the north, the village of Mahon owed its existence to the Wabash & Erie Canal. Mahon was settled by Irish men working on the canal and quickly became a boom town. Samuel Mahon—one of four brothers associated with the community's founding—became a prominent partner in canal commerce. He was part owner of the Wabash & Erie Transportation Company that operated canal boats and stage coaches from the then-terminus of the canal "at a point in Ohio, six miles beyond the Indiana State Line," according to an 1841 advertisement.

In his 1921 reminiscence, Dr. Koontz pointed an accusatory finger at an unnamed individual of "some wealth and a vast store of self-esteem" for persuading the railroad "to make a circle around Roanoke and again strike the southwestern tour immediately below the town." The individual profited by having the railroad run through his land along the eastern side of the canal. Koontz said Roanoke was unfairly treated because the town "found itself entirely unable to subscribe the amount of money exacted" by the railroad company. In a passage marked by some uncommonly ascerbic comments, he added:

> So the circle was made making Mahon a point on the road and leaving Roanoke a mile off in the country, giving Mahon . . . a temporary boom and Roanoke a similar back set. With a railroad and a depot, our lord and master could safely prosecute his favorite project and assume municipal affairs unmolested, and Mahon soon boasted of a grist mill, saw mill, store, distillery and most important of all, a prosperous saloon, which of course required no effort or advertisement on the part of its proprietor to induce a patronage. But like the famous Mississippi bubble, the boastful Mahon bubble also burst and the station was moved to its antagonist, the town of Roanoke, and all the trains ceased stopping at his front door. So if his lordship found it necessary to make a trip on the railroad, like his fellow townsmen he was forced to the humility of tucking his pant legs into his boot tops and wade the waves of mud and water to the depot two miles away.

In the end, Mahon slowly disappeared while Roanoke continued its economic growth.

By 1889, after several mergers and reorganizations, the Wabash Railroad Company consisted of more than thirty-five hundred miles of track. It served Roanoke from a freight spur at the Roanoke Elevator Company and a small passenger station that was operated by Samuel Zent after its completion in December 1880, on Station Street southeast of town. But the passenger service for Roanoke wasn't as robust as the canal had provided in its heyday. The *Wabash Cannonball* passenger train made famous by the poem and folk tune rumbled and roared through each day without stopping, while two lesser renowned trains—the late-afternoon *Detroit Limited* and the nighttime *St. Louis Limited*—called at Roanoke for many years.

The Wabash participated in the mammoth movement of troops and materiel during World War II, alongside other renowned railroads serving northern Indiana such as the Pennsylvania, the New York Central, the Baltimore & Ohio, and the Nickel Plate Road.

The shriek of the steam engine whistle was silenced on the Wabash by 1953, replaced by the horn of the diesel locomotive. The Wabash, like all U.S. railroads, suffered a catastrophic drop in passenger service during the mid-1950s as travelers opted for the independence of the automobile or the speed of the airplane.

By this time, Roanoke passenger service was downgraded to local (or "way") freights—freight trains that would couple on a passenger car or two. The westbound freight No. 71 had a "flag stop" in Roanoke at 7:40 A.M., while its eastbound counterpart, train No. 72, rolled through at 10:15 A.M. Roanoke travelers who wished to go by rail had to flag down these trains. The passenger timetable warned:

The Roanoke Elevator began serving the area's farmers at the Wabash Railroad stop one mile east of the town in 1922. It is one of the oldest continually operating businesses in Roanoke. With the demolition of the old railroad station, it is the lone reminder of a time when Wabash passenger trains stopped in Roanoke.

The Wabash Railroad Company does not wish to carry passengers upon way-freight trains, and does so only as an accommodation to the public. These trains cannot stop at the station platforms, and all persons who ride on them do so with the understanding that they must get on or off where the cars may chance to stop, and that they assume all inconvenience and risk in getting to or from the cars.

When you talk with longtime residents of Roanoke today, they share memories of catching the train to Chicago from Fort Wayne rather than boarding a train in Roanoke and then having to change at another station to make a connecting train. The last printed timetable to carry a Roanoke stop for the Wabash was dated October 30, 1955.

The Wabash was absorbed by the Norfolk and Western in 1964. Roanoke was never reinstated as a passenger stop and had to be content in hearing the passenger trains whistle by until Amtrak absorbed all of the nation's passenger rail routes. The famous *Cannonball* passed through Roanoke on its last run from Detroit to St. Louis on April 30, 1975. The freight spur was abandoned in the late 1970s and the long-vacant railroad depot on Station Street was razed less than a decade later. All that remains today are the elevator and the concrete slab on which the station rested. A merger in 1982 united the Norfolk and Western with the Southern Railway. The resultant Norfolk Southern still operates freight trains on the line east of the Little River with long lines of boxcars, domed tank cars and automobile carriers bound for distant cities.

The Interurban

Industrial development did not only affect farmers' markets and the way they marketed, it also changed their lives. Farm families found a swelling cornucopia of factory-made goods available to them, either in the local towns or by mail order. Farmers could buy ready-to-wear clothing, furniture, carpets, art works, musical instruments, toys, draperies and hundreds of other items. They no longer needed to construct their fences from hand-wrought rails, when barbed wire could be purchased, or to build homes, when Sears, Roebuck offered prefabricated models.

— David B. Danbom, *Born in the Country: A History of Rural America*

ANOTHER SET of tracks ran into the heart of Roanoke at the beginning of the twentieth century: the electrified "interurbans." The arrival of the new century saw the electrification of cities and then towns in large parts of America. Electric lighting became commonplace, replacing oil and gas lamps, and "labor-saving inventions"— as they were called then—took root. It was not long before farm wives and homemakers in towns like Roanoke wanted electric-powered fans, toasters and

Victrolas. Electric-powered transportation was championed in Indiana with the state capital being the hub for most interurban lines.

Wabash, Peru, and Logansport proved to be significant in terms of Roanoke's daily life. Interurbans were faster and more comfortable than travel by horse-drawn buggy. Moreover, inclement weather was less of a problem. The interconnectivity of the electric railways allowed town residents to travel to not only Fort Wayne and Huntington but also to distant cities like Indianapolis and Cincinnati for family social occasions or for special purchases.

In many ways the interurban brought Roanoke under the influence of Fort Wayne, just as many other small towns found themselves pulled into the gravitational field of larger cities. Fort Wayne had started a street railway system in 1871. The first streetcars were horse-drawn, but these were replaced over the next two decades by cars with electric motors. Soon a network arose to link adjacent cities and towns. Workers could commute to Fort Wayne for jobs at the large factories that were taking hold in the Summit City. It also brought more salesmen from prominent companies to sell manufactured goods and food products to the Roanoke stores.

In 1901 rails were laid along the old canal towpath and into Roanoke for the cars of the Fort Wayne and Wabash Valley Traction Company. An electrical substation for the overhead wire to power the interurban cars was built near where the Dickey Lock had stood. By the 1920s, ten interurbans bound for Huntington and ten more headed to Fort Wayne stopped at Roanoke daily.

Cleaner and quieter than a steam train, the interurban was an elegant way to travel. The Roanoke column in the *Huntington Weekly Herald* often mentioned the relatives of residents had "Sundayed" in the town, using the interurban as their means of travel. The electric-powered streetcars provided more than transportation of workers and visitors to Fort Wayne and Huntington. They also provided a means to

The interurban served Roanoke for more than thirty years, connecting residents with larger cities with a cleaner and more comfortable form of transportation. The interurbans were replaced by buses in the 1930s, which did not use the Roanoke depot.

Above: Interurban 296 of the Fort Wayne and Wabash Valley Traction Company shown at the Roanoke station in 1912. The sixty-one-foot-long car was one of seven luxury parlor-buffet cars on the Fort Wayne-Indianapolis route that stopped in Roanoke. (Bob Rose illustration)

Right: A speeding, empty interurban from Indianapolis failed to wait at a siding and crashed into the southbound Fort Wayne Flyer in May 1924, killing five people and injuring many others.

ship goods, because many of the interurbans hauled freight directly to the town. An advantage of the interurban was that it was inexpensive. Even in its later years, the cost for riding the interurbans was only one and a half cents per mile.

Interurbans were also safe in comparison to other forms of travel. In 1937 the local interurbans advertised that they were the way to "Avoid Highway Hazards. Don't take any chances when you travel." Ironically, one of the worst accidents to occur within Roanoke's history occurred on the interurban line in May 1924, when five people were killed and many injured when the *Wabash Valley Flyer* from Fort Wayne crashed head-on into an empty interurban that had failed to wait at a siding. It was estimated the *Flyer* was traveling at thirty-five miles per hour when the accident occurred near the site of the Roanoke Creamery. The accident attracted spectators by the hundreds. Volunteers directed traffic, as each intersection in town became jammed with vehicles.

But just as the canal was made prematurely obsolete, so was the interurbans' period of popularity curtailed. Even before 1925 when it carried fifty million passengers, the interurban industry showed signs it was trying to grow beyond its means. Too many interurban lines and too little supporting capital were major contributors to their downfall. The railroads proved to be a more efficient means of transportation for freight and for passenger travel of more than fifty miles. Another cause for its demise was Henry Ford and his revolutionary assembly line production process. By 1925 Ford had sold more than ten million Model Ts (costing $275 apiece) across the nation. The interurban was doomed and replaced by buses.

An effort to save the electric village-to-village streetcars in Indiana in the 1930s was quashed by the Depression. The interurbans stopped running to Roanoke by 1938. Few traces of the old Roanoke interurban can be found today. Although most of its route was paved over by U.S. Highway 24, part of the roadbed can be seen south of Redding Drive closer to Fort Wayne, where a path through the woods and a series of telephone poles mark the route over which the streetcars clattered. The only other reminder is the Roanoke electrical substation, which contributed to the town's development after the interurban had disappeared.

Memories of interurban travel persist among older residents. Ralph W. Hine said his father came to an unexpected realization early in his marriage thanks to the village streetcars. The elder Hine worked on the interurban to and from Fort Wayne and he would often wave at folks along the way, particularly the pretty young women. After he was married, the senior Hine was talking about the interurban when he learned that one of the young girls he used to wave to as the streetcar passed West Hamilton Road was now his wife.

Interurban mass transit gave way to the bus and, more significantly, to the rise of the affordable passenger automobile. As in earlier times, Roanoke adapted and prospered with the newer means of transportation. It continued to serve a large area with its mills and stores. Roanoke was, according to a late-nineteenth-century history of the county, "a chief source of supplies for a large area of Huntington, Allen, and Whitley counties being at the time the principal trading place between Fort Wayne and Wabash."

The tenor of the town was captured by Will T. Lambert, editor of the *Roanoke Review*, in June 1904 when he wrote:

> Roanoke is ahead of its sister towns because it is no grave-yard; it is no place for men who are in business because they think it is more of a snap than other kinds of work; but it is the home of people who must hustle. It is the character of the individual that goes to make up the character of the community. Also, the stranger will be impressed with the fact that the citizens of Roanoke work for and believe in the town.

The perception of Roanoke as a hustling town persisted well into the twentieth century.

THE HIGHWAY

> The automobile solved the problem of short-range transportation. Railroads had connected major cities without seriously affecting local transportation, but highways served another purpose. They bridged the gaps existing in the railroad structure and rounded out the city's hinterlands. . . . Country towns are still adjusting to this tremendous revolution.
> — Lewis Atherton, *Main Street on the Middle Border*

WHILE THERE can be no doubt today that the automobile has changed the face of America, there was little inkling of its impact on Main Street in the small towns of America in the early 1900s. The automobile brought America to the doorstep of small towns through greater freedom of travel and accessibility. Then it took these benefits away, bypassing the small towns and leaving them to wither and decay. Roanoke was a classic case of boom and then bust, in large part because of the passenger car and the truck.

Roanoke's dirt roads were used by more than local residents seeking to buy and sell goods. The first legally established highway in the county ran northwest from Huntington to Fort Wayne. It was known as the Fort Wayne Road and went through downtown Roanoke. This made the town more than a crossroads marketplace that many other small communities in central Indiana became. Roanoke was a community that travelers came to recognize, using its amenities, including early hotels, restaurants and, of course, service stations. Evidence of the increasing attractiveness of the town can be found in an out-of-town newspaper praising a grocer named Alex Cressinger for adding "a nice and neat restaurant where the wants of the inner man can be supplied at all times."

The town's visibility was enhanced by its "improvements"—service stations, hotels, and tourist homes. Even today, if you want to start a debate among the older members of Roanoke, all you have to do is ask how many gas stations were located on

Main Street. The responses run from seven to ten, depending on the age and the recall of the citizen, for the 1.2-mile center of the town.

To the traveler, Roanoke seemed to be an active, prospering community. Merchants strove to make a good impression. E. E. Richards, owner of the store of bearing his name, fought for concrete sidewalks, adequate street lighting, and brick paving along Main Street early in the century. Richards believed that dirt roads and wooden sidewalks were detrimental to the livelihood of the town. The roads and its travelers also made Roanoke seem less isolated. The potbellied stove in the corner of hardware store operated by his older brother, N. D. E. Richards, attracted not only farmers, townsfolk, and employees, but also salesmen from Cleveland, Louisville, and Chicago, who regularly stopped in to share some chewing tobacco as well as stories from their travels.

The automobile brought other forms of change. The town was, in many ways, self-contained in the early 1900s. Almost all of a family's needs could be acquired downtown from merchants who knew and cared for their customers. It was, as one elderly member of the community noted, a better time when a youngster could find happiness by running down to Main Street and "get three pennies of peanuts and two pennies of Red Hots." Eventually, though, the new mobility meant a townsperson could go to Fort Wayne, for instance, to make his or her purchases.

Some businessmen saw their livelihood change or dissipate. George Blum saw Main Street go from horses and buggies to stylish coupes. When he arrived in Roanoke in 1878 Blum went to work as a harness maker for S. B. Dinius, taking over the business firm when the owner died. There weren't any paved streets and only three brick buildings on Main Street. It was a time when the needs of the traveling public who "succeeded in getting through the mud of the streets were taken care of by the Eagle Hotel," according to one remembrance. While the conditions on Main Street

Road builders were at a premium in the early twentieth century. North Main and Second streets were contoured and paved with brick in the early 1900s, adding a patina of civilization to the town. The bricks remain today, beneath the current pavement.

The Roanoke streetscape was like that of many small towns in Indiana in the 1890s, dominated by the Victorian functional style for Main Street commerce. The buildings were long and narrow and during the period were often called "blocks," even though they were individual structures. In this photo, the Richards Bros. Hardware Store with its frame construction and high parapet is an exception.

Where once horses and buggies had filled the street, automobiles were now congregated so their owners could buy items at Wasmuth's (right) or wait for repairs across the street. Automobiles brought the phenomenon of parallel parking to small-town America, replacing the diagonal positioning warranted by the horse and buggy.

The term "mass marketing" had a different meaning at the turn of the twentieth century as this display of crates indicates. Main Street merchants throughout the years would place items outside their doors to entice passersby to make a purchase.

changed, old customs and ways of living die slowly. The rural nature of Roanoke did not fully disappear, and Blum was still a successful harness maker before he died at the age of seventy-seven in 1933.

While some families maintained the skills of the past, others who came to Roanoke adjusted and welcomed the future. The Zent family and the Hartley family became major contributors to the community, in part through the rise of the automobile. Jess and Elmer Zent began selling automobiles in Roanoke in 1914 before dividing their duties between sales and repair. A second generation of Zents— Robert and his brother Dwight—continued as a Ford dealer until the mid-1970s. Jess and Elmer Zent also capitalized on the growth in commercial entertainment made possible by the ease of transportation afforded by the automobile. Elmer Slater had built a baseball park at the north end of town at the turn of the century. The Zents purchased the property in 1921 and expanded the facility to include a covered grandstand that seated almost six hundred people. They renamed it Oak Grove Park and added other entertainment, including a grandstand and later a dance pavilion. It proved one of the area's most popular destinations, and a hotel was built on the site.

Glenn Hartley was a master mechanic and held patents on several devices including tractor steering mechanisms and a governor for Fordson Tractors. Glenn began his career with the Zents in their garage on Second and High Streets. He and his brother Ted—who was interested in building and driving race cars—opened a garage on North Main Street near Second Street in 1929 and operated there until 1962 when it moved around the block. A showroom was added eight years later. Today, Hartley's Garage is now the oldest continually operating business in Roanoke.

Ironically, the roads would prove to be a major contributor to Roanoke's decline in the second half of the twentieth century. The origin of the problem came when the Indiana State Highway Commission was established in 1917, sparking a debate over whether "through routes" or "local routes" should be given priority in financing. The Federal Highway Act was passed in 1925, creating the "U.S. Highway" system that set standards for construction as well as a uniform numbering system. State Route 7, which ran from Fort Wayne to Huntington through Roanoke, was renamed U.S. 24 in 1926, even though it had not been "hard-surfaced" over its entire distance. For a while the new federally financed improvements to the highway system brought an even greater stream of traffic through the town over the years. Longtime residents remember a steady flow of trucks and cars through downtown Roanoke. In 1941, with the United States' entry into World War II in the offing, the Federal Road Bureau addressed a strategic weakness in the nation's lack of long-distance highways. Neither men nor materiel could be moved quickly if—as was feared then—Hitler bombed America's railroad infrastructure. As part of a national program, it mapped a route from Fort Wayne to Roanoke along the old canal bed and parallel to the inactive interurban tracks.

What was good for the country had ominous overtones for the town. As early as 1937 some townspeople recognized what moving U.S. 24 away from Main Street would mean. That summer, traffic was detoured away from the center of town because of bridge repairs. In a front-page editorial, the *Roanoke Review* editor expressed the

The Zent family has been a prominent part of Roanoke since the 1850s, first in farming and then in business. Jess and Elmer Zent opened a garage on Second Street in 1914 (right), selling Fords. It was relocated to a distinctively styled building at Vine and Main (below) where it was run by the Zent family until June 1978.

The State Bank of Roanoke (above) was the only bank in town when this photograph was taken after a 1912 snowstorm. The bank's growth and the economic issues of the time led it to become the First National Bank of Roanoke in 1917.

Main Street businesses also included some manufacturing. Workers at the Wayne Knitting Mill plant in Roanoke (seen at left) produced a special form of hosiery that contributed to the Fort Wayne company's being very successful in the early 1900s.

townspeople's fears should the rerouting become permanent: "At the present time, Roanoke is located upon a good traveled highway with property and rent values on the increase. . . . Factories do not locate today in towns that are not on good highways, neither do substantial citizens buy or build homes in towns that are not so located." He pointed out that the four-week detour "greatly reduced the volume of business that is being done by our local business houses" and that it seemed such a reduction in retail business would lead to fewer stores. In turn, this would mean lost revenue for the community and a greater tax burden on residents. It was prophetic, albeit a bit premature because of the economic activity caused by World War II and the pent-up demand for products in the postwar years.

E. E. Richards, seen here in his office in the 1930s, was the consummate businessman. Ever active, he could be found in his place at his store until eleven days before his death in 1937 at the age of seventy-eight.

The 1889 wedding portrait of N. D. E. Richards and his bride, Emma Kelsey. Their life together was brief—in 1895 she died of tuberculosis at the age of thirty-two.

E. E. Richards & Sons

A Good Store

In a Good Town

WEEKLY PRICE BULLETIN

July 10, 1924

The Things You Need - At Right Prices - A Service With Merit

Watch for Richard's Bulletin in each week's Review. We will advertise our Special Sales only through this medium. Watch for them---They save you money

Dry Goods and Rugs	Groceries and Meats	Men's Furnishings and Shoes

Dry Goods and Rugs

Dry Goods Prices That Merit Your Attention

Plain Ratines for warm weather 59c regular, per yard _____ **39c**

45c Crepes, stripes and checks, undergarments, childs dresses, etc **29c**

Blouses with band or tuck-in, new **20% Discount**

3 Only, $65 Axminster Rugs, very heavy, extra value **$45.00**

One Lot New Tissue Gingham Dresses **$3.75**

Night Gowns and Combinations as cheap as 98c and **59c**

Groceries and Meats

Toilet Paper, 10c size, per roll . 5c
Glass Tumblers, jell or table, 6 for 19c
    Per dozen . . 37c
Fig Bars, 2 pounds for . . 25c
Ginger Snaps, 2 pounds . . 19c
Pen-Jell, 2 for . . . 25c
Van Camp's Pork and Beans, 3 for 25c
Little Quaker Corn, finest pack . 19c
Kitchen Klenser or Wyandotte, 2 for 12c
Scouring Powder, 2 cans for . 12c
Seeded or Seedless Raisins, pound 22c
Palm Olive Soap, 3 for . . 21c
Quaker Quick Cook Oats 10c and 25c
Good Salmon, tall cans, 15c, 3 for 42c

Men's Furnishings and Shoes

Furnishing Department

All Dress Straw Hats at_____ **25% Discount**

One Lot of Short Sleeve Play Suits, $1.25 value _____ **49c**

Shoe Department

One Lot Oxfords for Women values to $4.85 at_____ **$2.19**

All Men's $4.85 Oxfords Special only _____ **$3.85**

E. E. RICHARDS & SONS

THE BIG 4 DEPARTMENT STORE

ROANOKE, INDIANA

"I ALWAYS Pay My Debts!"

Of all the Liberty Loans, this is the most important.

We went in to win and to win quickly. We won. Now we have got to pay our bills.

It means we must see the thing through—Uncle Sam's debt is your debt and my debt.

Let's put over the Victory Liberty Loan with a bang and see the thing up—buy for cash and buy on installments and do it today.

Victory Liberty Loan Committee

This space contributed by

The State Bank of Roanoke

W. M. KOONTZ & SONS
Funeral Directors
Furniture   Pianos
Columbia Grafonolas and Records
Phones 3 on 82 and 1 on 82
Roanoke, Ind.

Small-town values can be seen in this selection of advertisements from the 1920s in Roanoke. Whether it was the State Bank's patriotic call to buy Liberty Loans, or the handy fan from Koontz's, the underlying message of Roanoke business can be seen in the "ears" of the E. E. Richards ad: "A GOOD STORE . . . IN A GOOD TOWN."

CHAPTER 4

PROSPERITY

ROANOKE IN 1920

Rural America inspired the "American Dream." That dream included independence, freedom, and opportunity. It included a certain peace, serenity, and satisfaction that came as a reward for honest effort. Contrary to today's concept of that dream, it was of middle-class proportions. It did not include continuous expansion, but rather of a farm that a family could manage, pay off a mortgage, and have a little to help the next generation. The merchants in those small towns did not dream of supermarkets and malls, but rather a business that would support a comfortable home and lifestyle. Both were content with comfort and security rather than great wealth and luxury.

— Charlie Cole, Indiana farmer and essayist

THE AUTOMOBILE helped propel the nation into the "Roaring Twenties," a time of speculative investments and postwar expansion. Social changes also were attempted, some more successful than others. The Volstead Act, which banned the sale of any beverage containing 0.5 percent or more alcohol, made Prohibition the law of the land effective February 1, 1920. While there were more than four thousand convictions across the country for rum running and the like in the first year, violent gangsters like Al Capone and Legs Diamond weren't prevalent until later in the decade.

In Roanoke and the rest of the nation, the after-effects of World War I were dissipating and a new era was beginning. It would bring with it many changes and challenges. The nation's debt to finance the war was almost under control, but the resultant inflation was not. President Woodrow Wilson's effort to institute a period of peace through the League of Nations was rebuffed in the U.S. Senate. The United States' absence would spell the eventual doom of the league.

Instead of international involvement, the nation was more intent on deporting Bolsheviks and anarchists. In August, Tennessee ratified what was then called the Susan B. Anthony amendment, raising the number of states approving the right of women to vote to thirty-six and thereby making it law. In November, the voters opted to "return to normalcy" with the election of Warren G. Harding as president. There also were rumors that the Chicago White Sox were involved with gamblers in their loss to the Cincinnati Reds in the 1919 World Series, but the Black Sox scandal wouldn't end up in the courts for another year.

There was no indication at the beginning of the decade of the desperate times that lay ahead. Indeed, 1920 Roanoke climbed aboard a growing wave of prosperity that would almost last a decade. From the first week in January when the E. E. Richards & Sons department store announced its semiannual clearance sale of the holiday specialties, Main Street was an active place for commerce. The *Roanoke Review* ran a banner that read: "Trade at Home—Merchandise Bought in Roanoke Always Gives Satisfaction."

The merchants along Main Street were pleased to have new products to sell after the War to End All Wars. Zent Brothers began 1920 counseling consumers interested in buying a Ford to make their decision immediately because the supply of cars was going to be limited. By midyear, availability was not an issue. The Zent Brothers were advertising Runabouts for $550; Touring Cars for $575; Coupes for $750; Sedans for $875; and Truck Chassis for $600. Mechanized farm equipment came into the market, too, with the Richards Brothers offering Samson Tractors and an entire line of International Harvester farm equipment. A. Wasmuth & Sons sponsored a one-dollar competition for anyone who could guess "why the people of Roanoke and vicinity would buy 116 Goodyear tires during the month of February 1920 compared with 14 tires during the same month the year before." The winning reason, Wasmuth reported a week later, was that "people have learned that Goodyear Tires give more miles for less money than any other tire." The fact that the nation was still on a wartime economy in 1919 and that fewer tires or tire-buyers were available then seemed to have been overlooked.

E. E. Richards & Sons offered a greater variety of men's and women's clothing as well as dry goods and groceries. Richards proclaimed you could have "a spotless, cheery kitchen" with the installation of Armstrong linoleum, while W. M. Koontz & Sons offered Napanee Dutch Kitchenettes at an affordable price. Even animal feed was abundant, and Wasmuth's crowed about the better results available if you used Purina Chick Feed and Purina Chicken Chowder with your hens. L. A. Eddingfield & Son offered rubber goods like boots as well as groceries, sweaters, shoes, corsets, underwear, dry goods and hosiery. Fisher Brothers restaurant invited diners to come in and enjoy "oysters any style."

There were other signs of prosperity. The Roanoke Telephone Company, originated in 1892 by E. E. Richards and E. M. Wasmuth, served several hundred homes. One of the first "automatic" exchanges in the nation, the Roanoke Telephone Company was located downtown, capable of serving up to twenty telephones. Among the first subscribers was Dr. J. W. Kemp, who had a phone at his home and office. But

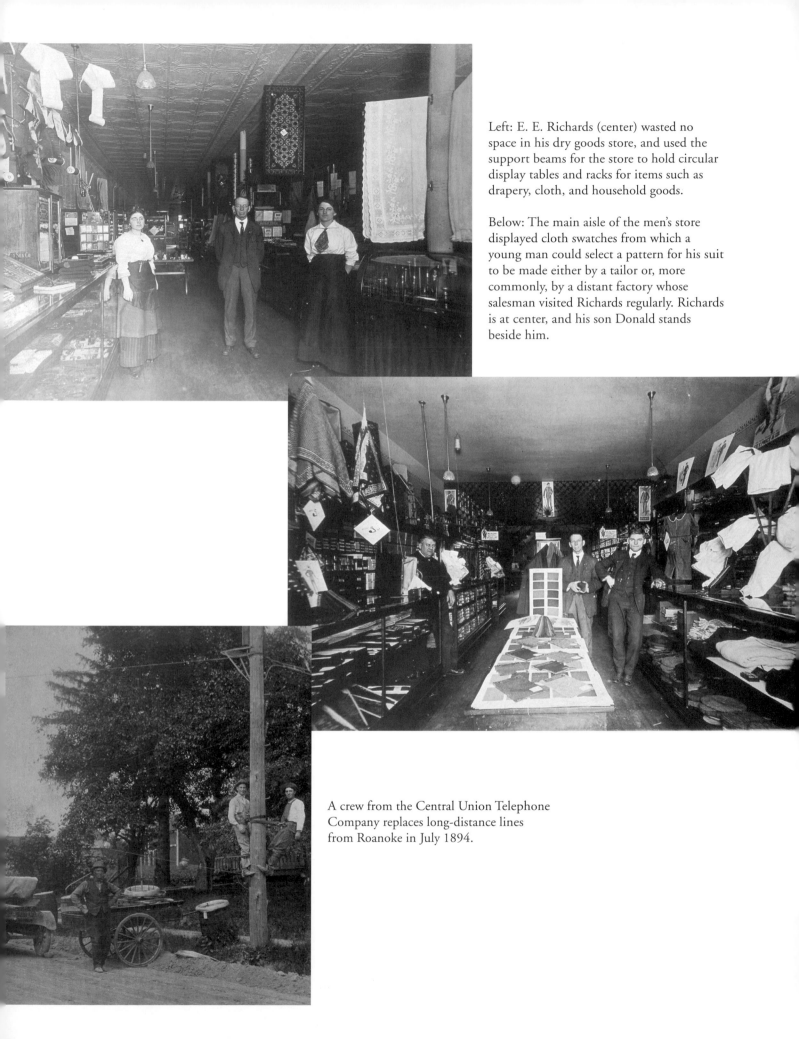

Left: E. E. Richards (center) wasted no space in his dry goods store, and used the support beams for the store to hold circular display tables and racks for items such as drapery, cloth, and household goods.

Below: The main aisle of the men's store displayed cloth swatches from which a young man could select a pattern for his suit to be made either by a tailor or, more commonly, by a distant factory whose salesman visited Richards regularly. Richards is at center, and his son Donald stands beside him.

A crew from the Central Union Telephone Company replaces long-distance lines from Roanoke in July 1894.

like many new inventions, the automatic exchange frequently failed and a manual switchboard was installed in 1895 in the home of Mrs. Jennie Hart, the town's first telephone operator. It was later moved back to the Richards' buildings before being sold to a Hicksville, Ohio, man in 1915. When it was purchased by the Home Telephone & Telegraph Company of Fort Wayne in 1928, the Roanoke system served more than four hundred phones. The purchase price was twenty-five thousand dollars.

Many of the townspeople were thriving and busy. Fraternal and civic organizations like the Masons and Odd Fellows had large gatherings. A Chautauqua in June 1920 brought prominent orators and musicians to the town for a three-day festival of learning and amusement. Equipment was secured and the first outdoor free "picture show" was held that summer with the movie projected on the north side of the Rindchen building on Main Street. Another indicator that more discretionary income was available was evident when the Purvis Drug Store on the corner of Main and Second streets proudly advertised the American walnut-encased Rich Tone Phonographs. Their cost was a hundred dollars and up. Later in the year, the Roanoke Volunteer Fire Department had a benefit concert featuring Ada Jones, a "famous phonograph artist" known for her "soubrette" (or coquettish) and "ragtime" songs. Readers of the weekly *Roanoke Review* relished the serialized versions of novels, including Edgar Rice Burroughs' *Tarzan and the Jewels of Opar*.

There were somber moments, too. The body of Army nurse Grace Buell was brought home at the end of March. The first Huntington County woman to die in World War I, she had contracted spinal meningitis in October 1918 at a base hospital in Portsmouth, England. All the stores closed at noon for the Decoration Day observance that year.

Some stores did not fare as well as others. L. E. Thomas, who had operated the Roanoke Bakery and called upon customers to "Eat Mother's Bread and Back Roanoke," sold his business in midyear to Pond & Good, who said that "with your support we are here to stay." Duhammel & Carpenter operated a restaurant that touted its "fresh fruit, ice cream, cakes, and canned goods" as well as tobacco products. In September, a fire gutted the restaurant and put it out of business. The two banks in town at the time—the First National and the Farmers' State—competed closely for customers. The banks ran weekly ads about their respective strengths. With its modern burglar alarm system and safe deposit boxes, the First National capitalized on the growing fear of crime in America. In one ad, it noted that the recent robbery at the Exchange Bank in nearby Churubusco was devastating to depositors there. The clear message in the ad was that "it couldn't happen here."

The year was a time of other changes for Roanoke, thanks to the efforts of a younger generation of community leaders. A committee of D. A. Wasmuth, A. A. Richards and Harry Dinius convinced the state to include Main Street as part of the new State Road 11 which ran from Greenfield in Hancock County to the main highway that connected Bluffton and Fort Wayne. The town's future in this first age of confident consumerism seemed secure.

Even a century apart in time, these photographs of Roanoke's North Main Street show the resiliency of the townscape. The row of brick buildings constructed by E. E. Richards in 1899 has been restored to the original handsomeness of Victorian Functional architecture. Instead of a grocery, dry goods store, and meat market, the buildings now contain offices of American Specialty.

Taken twenty years apart, these photographs show some of the changes on Roanoke's North Main Street, with the addition of landscaping and old-fashioned streetlights as well as careful restoration of the buildings. The old bank building and the former bakery (right) have been given a bright facelift and now house the gourmet restaurant, Joseph Decuis.

Maintaining the dignity of history can have its pleasant outcomes. Alice and Pete Eshelman (below) pose in the renovated bank building, seen on the facing page, that is now part of Joseph Decuis, which was established by American Specialty in 2000. The photo at left shows Nathan Highlands, cashier of the First & Farmers Bank, in October 1932, and his daughter, Mayme Highlands Henline. Nowadays, instead of storing cash and safe deposit boxes, the bank's vaults are used as a cigar humidor and wine cellar. The bank alarm, seen on the rear wall in both photographs, is still operational.

This site was the center of activity for more than a century for the town of Roanoke. The original Richards Bros. Hardware Store began operating here in a small one-room building in 1889. It was replaced by this brick structure in 1905 and remained an archetypal small-town hardware store until 1990 when it began its "second life" as the home of American Specialty.

Over the years, Roanoke's commercial area was focused along North Main Street with groceries, pharmacies, and department stores serving the needs of the area's residents. Today the buildings constructed by E. E. Richards serve as offices for the more than 150 American Specialty employees.

After its demise in 1924, the Farmer's State Bank building served as a furniture warehouse and a restaurant before becoming a photographer's studio and gallery. The overhead wires and signage of the 1980s, seen below, detracted from the Classic Revival architecture of the building. The bright cloth awnings installed in 2003 call to mind earlier times on Main Street.

Major renovation work transformed the interior of the nineteenth-century buildings into modern office space. The American Specialty boardroom (top) needed extensive work to replace a leaky roof and water-damaged flooring. The company lobby (center) is now a bright, airy entry with display cases of sports-related items. The fitness center (right) is housed in the former Odd Fellows hall, where employees work out regularly. A majority of employees participate in lifestyle fitness programs.

Above: Christopher C. Mulkins (1853–1947) used his childhood memories of Roanoke to produce this painting of the Wabash & Erie Canal's Dickey Lock in the 1930s. The painting shows the lock, Lemuel Jones' water-powered mill, and the turnabout as a canal boat approaches.

Left: Roanoke is a town with a young population. More than 40 percent are under the age of thirty. The town's growth—as with many small towns during the 1990s—can be attributed to a less hectic lifestyle, a short commute to nearby jobs, easy access to outdoor activities, and a sense of community that is stronger than exists in cities.

Below: The founders of American Specialty pose on North Main Street in Roanoke. From left are Dave Harris, Tim Eshelman, and Pete Eshelman, who located their fledgling company in an old hardware store in 1990 and have helped revitalize the town through their steadily growing business ever since.

The Roanoke Patriotic Pops concerts are among the most popular summer events for families in northeastern Indiana. Spectators crowd onto a block-long section of Main Street to hear popular and classical American music played by the Fort Wayne Philharmonic each July Third. Among the young and old alike who enjoyed recent concerts are (clockwise from bottom right): American Specialty president and CEO Pete Eshelman and Congressman Mark Souder; Honored World War II veteran Joseph Merckx; Rich Pape; Air National Guard Colonel Perry Collins and his wife, Clare; Jon and Tracy Goetz and their sons Karl and Seth; Patty Radcliffe; and John Nelson greeting another honored World War II veteran, Ralph Hine and wife, Ruth.

Roanoke's Early Civic Leaders

Roanoke has been graced with many business leaders during its history—men and women who found satisfaction in supplying the public with its needs. From its early days, the town has been known for its successful merchants on Main Street. The October 23, 1879, *Huntington Democrat* praised "clever, active and wide-awake" businessmen whose stores attract "a large and liberal patronage from the people of the surrounding country." Even the town's two saloon keepers—D. W. Rose and T. H. Pickle—came in for praise in the Huntington paper. Yet, the strongest praise was reserved for Windle & Wasmuth, described as a solid and reliable firm whose business "could illy be spared from the thriving town."

WASMUTH

This community respect for the Wasmuth name was still evident thirty years later. This was a considerable period of time for a business to remain successful in the late nineteenth century when the economy was frequented by financial crises.

> Perhaps the greatest impetus to the growth of Roanoke in recent years has been the character of the Wasmuth family. Other businessmen there are in good numbers of character and ability. E. E. Richards has a really metropolitan store. Richards Brothers are hustlers and a score of others might be named. Charles Koontz with a bakery and a restaurant that does an enormous business and the equally enterprising drug store of the Hacketts. But the State Bank of Roanoke has grown out of the enterprise by the Wasmuth family and it certainly does do a lot to finance the enterprises of Roanoke.
>
> A big hardware store, a lumber yard, grain elevator and mill and a number of other enterprises, among them the sale of automobiles continue to keep members of the family busy.
>
> — *The Evening Herald*, July 3, 1909

The landmark of one of the first captains of industry in Roanoke still stands at 212 North Main Street, one of the oldest brick building in the business community. The three-story structure that now houses Carroll's Furniture was once topped with the "W" cornice of Windle & Wasmuth, which not only offered agricultural implements and hardware, but also established the town's original banking institution.

The family scion was Augustus Wasmuth who emigrated to the United States from the German state of Westphalia in the mid-1850s at the age of fourteen. Like many men who rose to prominence, Wasmuth came to Roanoke from Stark County, Ohio. (Others include Jacob Zent, John Dinius, Daniel Richards, and Peter Grim.) Wasmuth spent four years of indentured service to a farmer in Stark County and moved to Roanoke in 1860. He was among the earliest to enlist from the town in the Union Army and fought in the Western campaign under General U. S. Grant. When he returned to Roanoke, he worked in Josiah

Grim's store. Using some of his military pay and his savings to open a store with W. K. Windle in April 1867, he began a partnership that would endure twenty-four years. In the same month, Wasmuth married Ellen Grim, a niece of his former boss.

The name Windle & Wasmuth proved synonymous with some of the best agricultural implements of their time. The business grew substantially with the opening of a sawmill—whose three-story, gray-brick building still stands to the north of McPherren Ditch—and the addition of hardware and other supplies in buildings at North Main and Third streets. Photographs from the late-nineteenth century show a grain mill in the midst of the Windle & Wasmuth complex as well. But it was with the banking business that Wasmuth met the vital needs of the community.

Established as a small private bank in 1878, the Bank of Roanoke was carefully shepherded by Wasmuth through the nation's financial panics of the 1890s. In 1908 it became the State Bank of Roanoke and the business occupied a prime location on Second Street, just east of Main. The bank grew and, in the face of some new competition, it prided itself as "The Old Bank" offering 4 percent on savings accounts. In 1915 Wasmuth brought in other investors and increased the bank's invested capital, whereupon the State Bank of Roanoke unveiled plans for a grand new building on the southwest corner of Main at Second. Two years later, the classically designed limestone structure was opened. In 1919 the bank was converted into a national bank and Wasmuth became chairman of the board as his son, Daniel A. Wasmuth, assumed the presidency. The First National Bank was the larger of the town's two banks and absorbed the Farmer's State Bank when it was liquidated in February 1924, becoming the First and Farmer's Bank. Augustus Wasmuth died in 1923, but his family—which included seven children— remained prominent in the town, the county and the state. Daniel A. Wasmuth was president of the bank until it closed in the Depression. Another son, Edmund Wasmuth, rose to president of Kitchen Maid Corporation in Andrews after the family bought that business in 1911. He was twice elected to the state legislature from Roanoke and was elected state Republican chairman in 1918 and 1920. In 1924, Wasmuth had to quell a grassroots movement to nominate him for governor.

DINIUS

Across Main Street from Wasmuth's building was the site another prominent family business begun by one of the early settlers. John J. Dinius came to Roanoke in 1851 from Stark County, Ohio, crossing the Great Black Swamp with a family of three boys and three girls in an ox-drawn wagon. Dinius established a tannery, utilizing the great supply of white oak bark needed for the process of converting hides into leather. The tannery off Third Street continued for many years under the direction of Henry Dinius. John Dinius's oldest son, Solomon, learned the harness trade and developed a business that operated for many years. Another member of the Dinius family, Harry Dinius, went on to become manager of A. Wasmuth & Sons Co. and eventually assumed its lumberyard and coal yard business under his own name. These two families—Wasmuth and Dinius—thus played integral roles in the development of Roanoke for six decades.

★

KOONTZ

There were many excellent businessmen and businesswomen in Roanoke in the early 1900s. The Koontz family viewed the growth of the town from a unique perspective: A. P. Koontz came to town in the antebellum period as an apprentice to a furniture maker and became the town's lone undertaker. After the Civil War, he built the first horse-drawn hearse in the county. His son William continued what by then had become a furniture-selling rather than furniture-making business into the twentieth century. In turn, his sons joined the firm after serving in World War I and they purchased the Wasmuth Hardware Store on the northeast corner of Main and Second streets.

By the 1930s, William Koontz and Sons was the only business still in the hands of the descendants of an original founding family. There were many other business leaders: John C. Nussdorfer, who was a barber and Fire Department chief, and Lawrence Eddingfield, whose general merchandise store occupied the northwest corner of North Main and First streets. They were symbolic of the commitment businessmen made to the community in both post-Civil War mercantile boom and the advent of the automobile in the 1920s.

★

RICHARDS

But one name resounded along Main Street, perhaps more than all the others, and that was "Richards."

Daniel Richards, his sons and his grandsons all played key roles in Roanoke's commerce through their stores and their advocacy of the community. Their span can best be understood through the products they sold. When E. E. Richards opened his first store in 1884 and his brothers, Marvin and Newton D. E. Richards, opened their one-room store under the name of Richards Brothers in 1889, they served a customer base that traveled by horse and buggy and lit their homes with gas lamps. In time, they replaced their small buildings with brick structures that have withstood the test of time on Main Street. They were influential in the growth of the town and its administration. They served on boards for governmental, civic and religious organizations, shaping the fabric and the future of the community.

Upon the fiftieth anniversary of his business, N. D. E. Richards reflected that his store's success was attributable to its carrying "a complete, diversified, up to the minute line of merchandise." The ultimate critical factor, he said, was to impress both his regular and transient customers that he was fully prepared to meet their needs.

CHAPTER 5

DECLINE

In many cases, one often finds towns with boarded-up facades—streetscapes that have, in effect, closed down—where commercial trade has shifted, either to other parts of town or farther away . . . towns where Main Street appears as if the merchants "just up and walked away," as one old-timer put it, in a relative short time.

— Richard V. Francaviglia, *Main Street Revisited*

THE DEPRESSION was hard on Roanoke, as it was on towns and cities through the country. The townspeople who lived through it will tell you that they were poor, but not hungry, pointing to the community's many farms and gardens. Doctors, for example, were sometimes paid in farm produce or hunted game. They also note that families stuck together in the face of adversity. That may be true in the overall sense, but there also were many families who struggled to survive during the period. Even the weather seemed to be more adversarial during the Depression. There was serious flooding in Roanoke on at least two occasions. In February 1936, a prolonged cold spell left the town stranded. Roads leading to community were covered with ice, forcing the closing of the school because it was without coal to heat the building. In addition, the water service lines on the west side of Main Street were frozen for more than a week, leaving many homes without water.

As in many small communities, Roanoke did its best to offset the impact of the Depression as it worsened. Businessmen on Main Street fought fiercely to maintain their businesses. Bakers, insurers, café proprietors, and service-station operators all banded together to tout the town's attractions by sharing advertising costs in 1932. A year later, the merchants launched a "Cooperative Sales" program to make readers of the Roanoke newspaper aware of the competitively priced goods for sale in the town. The Main Street Café advertised that its Sunday Chicken Dinner was just twenty-five cents. J. Thomas Ripley's grocery was selling hand-picked beans at six pounds for twenty-five cents and two dozen oranges for thirty-five cents. E. E. Richards store was offering men's denim overalls at fifty cents and children's shoes at ninety-five cents. In addition, the Main Street merchants kept their stores open Wednesday nights, and in order to attract more shoppers presented entertainment downtown. Velma Runyan was a longtime clerk for E. E. Richards and remembers the popularity of "sugar drawings" on Main Street. A customer at the store would write his or her name on the sales slip and place it in a jar. Large crowds would gather Wednesday evenings to see who won the five pounds of sugar. These sugar drawings continued until after World War II because rationing curtailed the supply of sugar.

It did not have the hoped-for effect. In May 1933, Roanoke newspaper editor C. M. Ervin used the front page of the *Review* to tweak the townspeople over their lack of support for downtown. Under the startling headline "SMALL TOWNS DON'T DIE, THEY COMMIT SUICIDE," Ervin criticized residents for shopping in places other than Roanoke. "When you spend a dollar outside, you take it right out of the pockets of some local citizen," he wrote. "If everybody who makes his money in this community would spend his money in this community, the home town would double in population in a few years and everybody in and around it would be prosperous.

"Why are filling stations out of proportion to every other line of business in number? Because people buy most all of their gas and oil at home," the editor maintained.

The Depression sent men and women searching for jobs in more distant places. Verlin Witherow was among a group of men who began working at International Harvester in Fort Wayne in the 1930s. Other men went farther afield to find work, such as the Studebaker plant in South Bend. Families found ways to survive. One family somehow operated an icehouse from a barn on High Street.

When war struck on December 7, 1941, many Roanoke men volunteered and found themselves traveling previously unimaginable distances. They rode troop trains

Roanoke's economy was hurt by more than the Depression. Flooding affected more than homes and businesses. As seen here, it also washed out bridges and tracks, resulting in overturned streetcars.

to distant camps and ports. Some fought in countries from which their ancestors had emigrated. Others went to war on Pacific islands whose names they'd never even seen on a map.

When the military men and women of Roanoke came home from World War II in 1946, most veterans say they found the town looking much the same. But there were changes beneath the surface. DeLoss Hartley, who served as a flight instructor during the war, remembers that the volume of traffic on Main Street dropped considerably when the new U.S. 24 was completed.

At the same time, townspeople were more willing to look for work beyond the town's limits than they were before. Wherever the destination, it could be more easily reached by automobile—whether it was for work or for shopping or for sightseeing with the family. Slowly, but surely, the ease of travel on the modern U.S. 24—which was expanded to a four-lane highway with a grassy median after the war—made its impact felt on Main Street businesses.

The development of the Time Corners shopping area fifteen miles from Roanoke began in the late 1940s, with a service station that also served as a country store. Nearby housing and traffic increased, bringing about some commercial development. In the early 1960s a Southern company purchased land to build a large supermarket, but went bankrupt before construction could begin. The Rogers family took over the project and with some modifications (the Southern company's blueprints called for segregated bathrooms. "That," W. W. Rogers said strongly, "won't happen here."), the store was built. By 1966 the eastern portion of today's Time Corners shopping center was completed and in use. By 1970 the Covington Plaza area was under development. Fort Wayne now seemed much closer to Roanoke than before. The Time Corners development has had a reverberating effect that is still felt today, as demonstrated by the construction of mega retail facilities along U.S. 24.

It is easy to suppose that Time Corners' impact was immediate, but it was not. A shopping trip to Time Corners in the 1960s was a "big deal," according to residents who were then in their teens and who found the modern, convenient stores there more attractive than the old row of brick buildings on Roanoke's Main Street. Later, large chain supermarkets and department stores came into prominence and underpriced the so-called "Mom & Pop" stores that were prevalent in communities like Roanoke. The 1960s, '70s, and '80s saw the Roanoke retail community fight a rearguard, and ultimately futile, action.

Bob Turpin, who with his wife Kolleen operated a grocery store on Main Street in the old E. E. Richards' complex in the 1980s, tells the story of working in his yard one day and noticing a neighbor driving around and around the block. When he was through in the yard and went in his house, Turpin happened to look out his window and see the couple's car pull into their driveway. There they hurriedly unloaded groceries that they had purchased from a larger supermarket in Fort Wayne.

"It's not that the competition offered better prices, because I checked and found that they were not," Turpin recalled. It was more basic than that: The newer stores marketed the fact that they were a new experience.

"There was a terrific selection of retail stores on Main Street when we opened.

There were stores selling kids' clothes, hardware, auto parts, a gift shop, a drugstore, an optometrist, the Village Inn Restaurant, a pizza parlor, an ice cream sandwich shop, and a laundromat," Turpin said. "The problem was that eventually we only attracted shoppers when they needed something and they would come down and buy that one item. When it came to those larger, profitable discretionary purchases, they took their dollars elsewhere." It was a pattern that was being duplicated all over small-town America.

Roanoke residents seem to agree on the one momentous event that sent the town into its decline: the county's consolidation of Roanoke and other small high schools into one large facility in Huntington. Roanoke had prided itself in its educational opportunities almost from its inception. Dr. Sylvanus Koontz recalled the first classroom for young people in a basement of a canal building. Frederick Reefy brought renown to Roanoke with the opening of the Classical Seminary—a private secondary school—in 1860. This led to the town being known as the "Athens of the County," a term used first by the *Huntington Democrat* in 1879.

The first public school was a large frame affair on Main Street at Eighth Street, one that was subsequently moved to First and High when it was decided that a brick structure should replace it. The current school on Vine Street was built in 1925 and enlarged in 1957. The high school classes were typical of small towns—few in number but large in spirit. Since they are Hoosiers and revere basketball, some residents will point to 1935 and 1936 when the Roanoke High School team won the Huntington Sectionals. More important, the high school served as the center of communal activity. A basketball game at home meant that the spectators would congregate in Roanoke's

Local heroes—the Roanoke High School basketball team won the 1936 Huntington Sectionals. Front row (from left): Ed Shaffner, Mel Hatter, John Schoeff, Charles Richey, and Wayne Thompson. Back row: Ernie Schoeff, Bob Ayers, Bill Koontz, Louie Zent, and Bill McPherren.

Bob Turpin

Not all of Roanoke's leaders arrived from Ohio in the nineteenth century, of course. There have been many individuals—educators, clergymen, and policemen—who have had a considerable influence on the town in the twentieth and now the twenty-first century. One of these is Judge Bob Turpin who has been a contributing member of the community since he arrived in 1978 from southern California with his family. Turpin, who was selected as "citizen of the year" in 2001 by the Roanoke Chamber of Commerce, owned and operated several businesses. He bought the then-closed Gary's Market on Main Street and turned it into a successful grocery in the 1980s. He later bought the old E. E. Richards buildings on Main Street and oversaw an antique mall. He also operated his own landscaping service.

In 1984 Turpin began what was to be an eight-year tenure on the Town Council, including service as its president from 1990 to 1992. This period proved to be one of the most tumultuous times in town history, as the community wrestled with the environmental issues associated with the C&M Plating properties. In retrospect, Turpin says it was a bleak time. It was the first time that environmental agencies had cracked down on a small business. It seemed to many in Roanoke a matter of over-reaction, especially as regulations changed and individuals were held accountable after the fact. Property values declined and a stigma descended upon the community.

Turpin and DeLoss Hartley found funding to ensure the quality of the water supply and to repair the waste treatment plant damaged by the plating company's dumping heavy metal waste into the sewage system. But the overall financial impact, Turpin says today, was "devastating."

In 1996 Turpin was selected to complete the term of Town Judge Margaret Moore, who retired. It was during Moore's tenure that the state enacted laws requiring towns to provide a municipal building for court meetings and a room in the town Utilities Building was designated for that

Judge Bob Turpin, 2002

purpose. At the time, the court saw sixteen to twenty-four cases daily with defendants, prosecutors, attorneys, families, and law enforcement officers crowded into one small room.

When Turpin took office, he was faced with implementing plans for a new court expansion in order to handle the increased caseload. With more than five hundred hours of volunteer help, the court facility was overhauled, equipped with computers to access records and with videotaping capabilities. Today the court handles more than seven thousand cases per year.

restaurants to talk about the outcome and the players. The opportunity for the community to experience its local identity in a spirit of social cohesion was lost when the Roanoke school lost its upper grades. As one longtime observer of the community said: "The end of Roanoke as we knew it came when they closed our high school in 1966 and moved it to Huntington."

Still, the changes on Main Street occurred slowly. The hardware store served a smaller and smaller clientele, and finally was open by appointment only. An antiques mall took the place of other businesses. The closing of the town's drugstore and impending failure of the remaining grocery store on Main Street seemed to leave townspeople with no choice but to shop elsewhere. The Village Inn appeared to be the lone commercial reason to drive into Roanoke.

Of course, this is not a unique story. Main Street merchants throughout America were decimated by large national corporations in the late twentieth century. What is different about Roanoke was that after its brush with disaster, the town experienced a remarkable recovery.

In 1987 the town faced one last, decisive crisis that was a near-fatal blow to its existence. The environmental furor over the C&M Plating Company represented a challenge more often associated with large manufacturing cities than with small rural communities. But rather than folding, Roanoke exhibited a determination that had become a trademark in its history.

Located at Main and Vine streets, the Continental Plating Company began operation in 1946 after purchasing and remodeling Ed Couture's Hi-Way Garage building. Ownership of the plating company changed hands over the subsequent thirty years before Martin and Dale John assumed control of the company in 1975. In an era of heightened environmental concerns, the Johns tried, but could not afford, to

Business leaders like DeLoss Hartley (left) rallied the town to resolve its environmental crisis. Hartley's father and uncle opened Hartley's Garage in the 1920s, and the family has been a significant contributor to the town's well-being ever since.

meet the new standards for use and disposal of hazardous materials. When it ceased operations in 1987, it was the town's largest employer.

In 1976 the company now known as C&M Plating was cited by state authorities for failure to meet standards for waste water. The company unsuccessfully tried to upgrade its treatment facility to meet the new environmental standards. In April 1983, another citation followed, this one for violation of federal pollution regulations. Three months later the state cited C&M for allegedly dumping pollutants—zinc, nickel, chrome, cadmium, oil, and grease—into Cow Creek. The company reported it had purchased additional pollution control equipment, and the state legal action was dropped.

C&M expanded its operation in November 1983, confident that its business would continue to grow. However, in April 1987, the Indiana Department of Environmental Management (IDEM) charged that C&M Plating's discharge was harmful to the town's wastewater treatment system. IDEM said C&M Plating was liable for more than four hundred violations of state regulations on disposal of hazardous wastes, maintaining environmental controls and falsifying records. Several months later, two hundred residents had to be evacuated because of a leak of hydrochloric acid from one of the C&M Plating buildings. The resultant damage to the town's wastewater treatment operation cost the town more than $1.2 million. The company stopped operations in late 1987 and filed for bankruptcy in 1990. It was not until late 1996 that the town had completed construction of a new waste treatment facility.

In 1995 a group of concerned citizens spearheaded by Perry Collins, E. J. Richards, and Steve Williams formed the Roanoke Economic Development Organization (REDO) as a nonprofit organization to work with environmental agencies in the cleanup and sale of the property. The ultimate goal was to eliminate this environmental hazard and eyesore and restore the properties to the Roanoke downtown and tax base.

With the aid of local volunteers, the buildings were razed and removed from the site at no cost to taxpayers. The huge volunteer effort was followed by a major remediation project spearheaded by the EPA with assistance from IDEM to remove contaminated soil and prepare the site for redevelopment. The project spanned almost five years, at a cost of about $2 million, and involved the cooperation of federal, state, county, local officials, and volunteers.

REDO took over the property in early 1999 from the county with the goal of finding the best use for the property as well as returning it to the tax rolls. In October 2002, the two-and-a-half-acre site was purchased by American Specialty, with plans to create a landscaped area which would provide much needed parking for the company's future growth and for downtown. Under provisions of REDO's charter, proceeds generated from the sale of the property will be used to help develop future economic development projects in the Roanoke area.

By the time REDO closed the chapter on Roanoke's environmental disaster, the renaissance of Roanoke was well under way. For the town, once again it was a familiar story of entrepreneurism on Main Street.

Roanoke's brush with environmental disaster began in 1987, when a metal-plating facility was alleged to be dumping hazardous waste into the town sewage system. On July 28, 1988, a tank containing approximately five hundred gallons of hydrochloric acid began leaking (above), prompting a major federal and state environmental action. This included pumping out storage tanks and drums on the site (left and below), as well as removal of contaminated soil. Eventually, the town razed the property through volunteer efforts and returned it to the tax rolls.

Flooding

For ninety years the creeks have played havoc with the town of Roanoke, especially the Main Street business section which is intersected by the two small streams. These streams—McPherren Ditch at Third Street and Cow Creek near Vine Street—have contributed to eighteen significant flooding episodes in nine decades, sometimes even when no rain had fallen on Roanoke.

In 1913, for example, a farmer who had built a new home on Third Street where the town parking lot is now located got out of bed one morning and found himself standing in water from the nearby creek. His daughter said that he sold the house quickly that summer and moved south of town.

The 1920s and 1930s saw newspaper headlines like "STREAMS ON RAMPAGE." Verlin Witherow wrote of wading up and down Main Street in the floodwater when he was a young boy in the 1920s. In March 1925, eighteen hours of continuous rain sent the Little River out of its banks, halting interurban service. Rains in January 1930 left the town marooned for several days. There was another serious flood in 1936 when the only way in or out of town was from the west.

It had hardly rained in town one Sunday night in June 1940 when Oscar Koontz looked out from his kitchen on West Fourth Street and saw a five-foot wall of water coming down the creek. A cloudburst northwest of the town caused the flood that turned Main Street into a river. Koontz's Furniture Store at Main and Second kept the floodwater from entering its building by stacking heavy furniture packing materials around the door. The Sandwich Inn on the west side of Main near First Street had several inches of water throughout and the workers at Zent's Garage had to stack batteries atop tables to keep them out of the eight inches of water in the building. A piano at Dibble's Café across the creek at 219 South Main was placed atop a Coca-Cola machine to keep it from being ruined. At the height of the flood, three feet of water at Main and Vine streets flooded the gasoline storage tanks of Zent, Schoeff, and Couture stations. Around the corner, Garretson & Son Feed Mill on First Street reported considerable damage to sacked feed.

Some memories about the floods in the early part of the twentieth century have their lighter aspects. Witherow, who was born in 1914, once wrote "we boys liked to see the floods come. We could launch a boat in the creek that used to be called Cow Creek, north branch, and end up in Huntington. Sometimes we would have to lie flat in the boat to get under the bridge. . . . I don't know how we every got by without someone drowning as we never had any flotation gear. We usually had to get Hartley's wrecker to haul the boat home because the current was too strong to row upstream."

The cause of the flooding lay in the rapid descent of the creeks just before entering the town. Water in the McPherren Ditch drops one hundred feet in less than two miles before reaching Roanoke, meaning a great deal of water hits the Main Street culvert at great speed. In addition, the Little River cannot handle a sudden onrush of water because it has not been adequately dredged over the years. When the town was young, many of the stores along Main Street were built above the water line.

The flooding didn't abate later in the century. The year 1996 was particularly hard on the town. In July, when the third flood had occurred within twelve months, the *Herald-Press* headline seemed to summarize the town's frustration: "SAME OLD STORY FOR FLOOD-WEARY ROANOKE." A total of five and a half inches of rain was recorded in less than twelve hours, bringing the creeks out of their banks and onto the streets. In the following winter, another flood was so strong that it washed away a retaining wall on Fourth Street.

The problem continued as the twenty-first century approached. Three inches of rain in less than thirty minutes in an April 1999 storm caused one reporter to write: "Noah might have felt right at home in Roanoke."

Main Street's location between two creeks that serve to drain thousands of acres of land into the Little River has meant frequent flooding. Residents worked feverishly with sandbags in an attempt to protect their businesses.

Nature's power can be awesome, as seen here by the strong current running south past Ambriola's Restaurant at First Street.

Sometimes even the best efforts couldn't keep the water out, as evidenced by the sodden flooring inside 212 North Main Street.

1670

1670 Miami Indians begin moving into northern Indiana with village near Roanoke.

1700 Europeans start to settle; conflict and Indian wars begin in Indiana.

1816

1816 Indiana becomes the nation's nineteenth state.

1835 The Wabash & Erie Canal opens connecting Fort Wayne and Huntington. A settlement develops around Dickey Lock that later becomes the town of Roanoke. Farmers enter the area.

1850

1850 Roanoke is platted by George Chapman with the first forty lots along canal and nine blocks on Main Street.

1856 Railroad reaches Roanoke with tracks one mile east of town.

1858 Classical Seminary, a private secondary school, is founded in Roanoke.

1871 First newspaper, the *Roanoke Register*, begins publication.

1874

1874 Town of Roanoke is incorporated.

1874 Long-abandoned Wabash and Erie Canal is officially closed.

1878 The Bank of Roanoke, Roanoke's first bank, is founded by Augustus Wasmuth and W. K. Windle.

1884

1884 E. E. Richards opens his first store, beginning a fifty-three-year retail career.

1889 Drainage project for Little River is completed, reclaiming about thirty-five thousand acres of swampland from Fort Wayne to Huntington.

1889 Classical Seminary leaves Roanoke and moves to North Manchester, where it becomes the forerunner of Manchester College.

1892 Roanoke Telephone Co. is founded by E. E. Richards and E. M. Wasmuth, bringing telephones to Roanoke.

1901

1901 Interurban streetcar service is extended to Roanoke from Fort Wayne.

1915 The Farmer's State Bank, Roanoke's second bank, begins operation.

1922 Jesse and J. Elmer Zent open Oak Grove Park featuring a hotel, tourist cabins, theater, merry go-round, tennis court, baseball diamond, picnic area, and grandstand for five hundred people.

1923 "Bon-Ton" pavilion is added to Oak Grove Park and remains in operation as a dance hall until 1942.

1924

1924 Roanoke's two banks merge to become First & Farmer's Bank.

1925 Roanoke School, providing grades K–12, is built on Vine Street.

1930 Oak Grove Park abandoned as victim of Depression.

1933

1933 President Franklin D. Roosevelt's "bank holiday" results in the First & Farmer's Bank being declared insolvent. Roanoke will not have a bank for another sixteen years.

1938 Interurban streetcar company goes bankrupt, ending service to Roanoke.

1941 Federal government relocates U. S. Highway 24 away from Main Street, shifting traffic away from Roanoke's downtown.

1949 Harmon Murbach and several Roanoke businessmen establish Roanoke State Bank, bringing banking back to downtown Roanoke.

1955

1955 Wabash Railroad ends passenger service for Roanoke.

1960s/1970s Town faces challenges of changes of shopping patterns.

1978 First National Bank of Huntington buys Roanoke State Bank.

1987 Federal and state environmental agencies charge C&M Plating with four hundred violations of state regulations creating environmental crisis.

Pete Eshelman, 2003

CHAPTER 6

Roanoke's Renaissance

We could see the town was in bad shape. The old buildings needed fixing. But this is a great employment area and our business basically relied on just telephones and airplanes. So we started here and, as we grew, we added on another building and then another. The town embraced our company. We were just a bunch of young guys starting a business, bringing jobs to the community, fixing up old buildings, becoming involved. We felt like we were making a good contribution to the town.

> — Pete Eshelman, *Fort Wayne News-Sentinel* interview,
> April 2002

★

1990

AMERICAN SPECIALTY ARRIVES

AT 5:20 P.M. on July 26, 1989, I was home after work and met my wife, Alice, on our back porch. At the same moment we both said, "I've got something to tell you," followed by "You go first—no, you go first" exchange. Alice told me she was pregnant with our third child. I gave her a big hug and said, "I've got great news, too. I quit my job today."

I could tell she was concerned—after all, we had a home, two children and one on the way, no job and no income. Even so, she was totally supportive. There was the obvious question about what were we going to do. I replied: "I'm going to start our own business, be my own boss, and pursue the American dream."

That was the beginning of our company. Fortunately, my friend Dave Harris had the same entrepreneurial itch and quit his job shortly thereafter, and his wife, Shirley, reacted in the same way as Alice did. My brother, Tim, was in Boston working in the insurance business, fresh out of the MBA program at Miami University of Ohio. We recruited him, and the three of us formed American Specialty.

Our business plan was simple: buck the traditional insurance industry's approach to managing risk and provide the sports-entertainment industry with a means to use the management of risk as a competitive advantage. Yes, we were taking on a huge, traditional industry. But why not? Sam Walton did, Bill Gates did, and so would Pete, Tim, and Dave.

On October 23, 1989, we officially started our business. My farm became our headquarters, and I converted my basement into an office. Our first client was the Milwaukee Brewers, the second was the Oakland As, the third was the American Power Boat Association, and then we began work with Major League Baseball. These clients remain with us today.

As we grew, we hired Taffy Troup, a Roanoke resident, as our receptionist, after she responded to our employment ad in the Fort Wayne newspaper. Taffy saw promise in us and in our basement business. Taffy is with us today, a vital member of my senior management team.

Leon Burrey, a retired engineer and handyman, worked for us part-time in whatever capacity we needed. I met Leon three years before while visiting the tack shop on his farm. Like Taffy, Leon today is an important member of our management team. His wisdom and ability to correctly read people has been invaluable to us.

Anyone who has brought employees into a home office knows the challenges. In addition to building an insurance business, employees learned the skills of babysitting and helping my kids with homework—but for me the commute was great. Fortunately, our business grew, and within six months we had outgrown the basement and looked for permanent office space. Tim, Dave, and I spent a lot of time deciding on a new location. We thought about locating our new business in obvious sports and entertainment centers: New York, Chicago, Orlando, Las Vegas, or Los Angeles. We ultimately decided to stay in northeast Indiana for "quality of life" reasons. We felt the area provided a great base of operation to raise families and businesses.

Insurance firm to ren

American Speciality Insurance may s

By JOHN KLINGENBERGER
Editor

A specialty insurance company -- which counts among its clients professional athletes and teams -- will be renovating a downtown building and moving here this summer.

Pete Eshelman, president of American Specialty Insurance Group, came before the Town Council last Tuesday night to outline his firm's plans for the former Roanoke Hardware. Eshelman said his company would close on that building -- among the oldest in Roanoke -- Tuesday, and begin restoration work immediately.

Eshelman, who was a pitcher in the New York Yankee organization and later a scout for the team, said his firm underwrites insurance for a host of professional athletes in the NBA, NFL and major leagues. In addition, the company offers insurance for a variety of sporting events. He described his line of coverage as "non-traditional" insurance, and explained that the company can offer short-term insurance for specific sporting

events, such as the Indiana major underwriters, he sai

Plans are to renovate making it into executive of which dates back to the 1 His company now include brother Tim Eshelman, Da

Eshelman said he was c location and size. "I've live cities. We (he and his wi southern Whitley County) Plus we have good access clients," Eshelman said.

Within two years, he a between 20 and 30 people. in specialty insurance wit last September. They cur

First we looked at nearby office parks, although these office parks seemed too expensive and too confining for our business, as we forecasted that we would experience tremendous growth. At breakfast one day, Leon came up with the idea of buying an old building for sale in nearby Roanoke and fixing it up. "Roanoke?" I asked. "It's a great place," Leon said, "five miles down the road, two restaurants, it's on the way to the airport, and inexpensive." The "on way to the airport" and "inexpensive" got our attention.

Alice and our two children had moved to Fort Wayne in 1986 from Boston. I had been in Roanoke only a couple of times, eating at its two restaurants. Ambriola's served good, home-style Italian food, and the Village Inn was the local neighborhood bar famous for its barbecued pork chops and broiled haddock. Our neighbors in Aboite affectionately said both the "mink and manure set" enjoyed the Village Inn. Other than those experiences, all I knew about Roanoke was that it was a little town off Highway 24 on the way to the airport.

The next day we drove to Roanoke, entering the town from the north on the old Roanoke Road. The first impression was not good. We saw houses and buildings in disrepair, some even boarded up. Sidewalks were crumbling, ugly streetlights and exposed overhead wires lined Main Street, and even the wooden trashcans on the sidewalks were ugly and falling apart. Roanoke looked like yesterday's news.

The old hardware store, however, seemed architecturally impressive. Large geraniums were growing in the front windows. A sign on the door said that hardware store was open only by appointment with the owner, Bob Humphries. In other words, the hardware business was slow. Leon called Bob and within five minutes he greeted us on Main Street, looked us over, and let us into the hardware store. The store was sparsely stocked with various hardware items. It had a classic tin ceiling, and the musty smell of my great-grandma's attic. As Bob showed us around, I realized he was checking us out more than we were checking out the store. He was intent on selling

ate hardware building

-30 new jobs in next two years

firm also works with other loyds of London.
floor of the building first, e first floor of the building, used for future expansion. ary officers -- himself, his d Leon Burrey.
Roanoke area because of its rk, Boston, and other major ome north of Roanoke (in eady for small-town living. eld here, for many of our

s the company will employ Harris have a background , and formed the company ut of offices in Columbia City.

The offices should be ready for occupancy by June 1, Eshelman said.

Roanoke Hardware was formerly operated by Bob and Sherri Humphries for the past 27 years. The Humphries sold their inventory at auction last month.

The announcement put to rest a lot of speculation about what would happen to the building. Local officials see Eshelman's plans as a boost to the entire community.

American Security is among a number of new businesses which have recently opened in Roanoke. Ironically, it was only a few months ago that local officials were concerned over the number of empty buildings, coupled with prospects that several other businesses would be leaving soon. In just a few short months, almost all the business buildings have been filled.

In addition, several new businesses will be opening soon, including a new convenience store and laundromat on U.S.-24.

The Roanoke weekly owned by the Quayle family, *Four Corners Courier*, welcomes the new firm in town in its April 11, 1990, issue.

only to someone who would respect the building. After all, he had owned the building for more than twenty-five years. I told him we were looking for space for our growing insurance business, and our intention was to remodel the building and preserve its character.

As we drove back to my farm, I "came to" and said, "Leon, what are we thinking of? The town is falling apart. Who would want to work for us, what clients would want to visit us in an environment like Roanoke?" Leon responded without hesitation, "Employees will work for, and business will come to, a great company—no matter where it's located. We are building a great company and we can afford the building." Of course, "afford the building" was the operative phrase.

Before making a final decision to purchase the building, we wanted to be certain we would not have problems with the town of Roanoke. Small towns have always been notorious for not liking outsiders. We presented our plan to convert the old hardware building into offices before the Roanoke Town Council. It proved to be a defining meeting. Leon displayed a wooden model of our proposed office made in the wood shop on his farm. After our brief presentation, the Town Council, to our surprise, unanimously approved our construction plans. Bob Turpin, president of the council, welcomed us to Roanoke, saying, "Your coming to town is one of the most positive things that has happened to Roanoke in the past several years. We wish you guys success and if the council can help you, please call on us." The council's enthusiasm and warm welcome convinced us to buy the building and move to Roanoke. Later we found out why our move to Roanoke seemed so positive to the local leaders. Downtown Roanoke was in the midst of crisis after crisis. Businesses were failing, and the environmental disaster created by C&M Plating had Roanoke postured for extinction. It couldn't have been worse for them or better for us. Timing is everything!

On May 2, 1990, we formally purchased the Roanoke Hardware Store. We had approached the contractor who had built my house to make the renovations. It turned out he was too busy with other projects to finish on our time schedule. Out of frustration, we turned to Leon, and he hired a local contracting company called Pape Construction. Rich Pape and his crew finished the job on time and our offices looked wonderful. Since that time, Rich and his crew (his wife, Karen, their son, Rick, Kevin Yoder, and Bob Sunday) have worked for us steadily and have been responsible for the renovation of the seventeen buildings that make up our corporate campus today. Rich and his family have become great friends, and without their efforts, the restoration and maintenance of our buildings would have been a management nightmare. When out-of-town guests comment on the craftsmanship of the outstanding renovations in Roanoke, I enjoy kidding Rich: "Pape who?" I'd say. "Tim, Dave, and I built all of this with our bare hands in our spare time."

Tim, Dave, and I spent evenings and weekends helping Rich and his crew remodel the old hardware store. We removed truckloads of junk and debris. To our pleasant surprise, several people from the town offered their assistance in carting the trash. When we offered money, they would not take it, saying they were just happy to help. We were overwhelmed by their generosity.

Tim, Dave, and I enjoyed helping Rich and his crew. Our efforts served the practical purpose of saving money by allowing us to put sweat equity into the project, but it also provided time to think and plan. When you put your heart, mind, and money into restoring a building, it becomes part of you and a source of tremendous pride and enjoyment.

We hired an interior designer, and Alice assisted her. We ultimately implemented most of Alice's suggestions, and as a result, Alice became our permanent interior decorator. Thirteen years later, she has been responsible for the interior and exterior design of our corporate campus. In fact, people in town have called on her for recommendations for improvements to their own buildings and homes.

On June 1 American Specialty's seven employees moved into the upstairs level of 142 North Main Street, Roanoke, Indiana, and we proudly declared it our corporate headquarters. The first floor remained vacant. In an effort to put something interesting in the first floor windows, Leon introduced us to Bob Zent, known around town as the town historian. Bob's family has lived in Roanoke for more than 150 years, and Bob has had a lifetime passion for collecting historical Roanoke items and chronicling Roanoke's history. Bob gave us old pictures of Roanoke, which we reproduced and displayed in the first-floor picture windows. This was the beginning of our interest in the history of Roanoke. The photos were so well received by townspeople that it inspired us to use Roanoke's history as the theme for future renovations.

We quickly grew and expanded our business throughout the first floor, occupying the entire building at 142 North Main. The garage attached to the building was used for parking and our fitness center. We accumulated some used exercise equipment,

The old hardware store awaits its new occupants in April 1990.

and made it available to employees and the Roanoke Volunteer Fire Department. This was the beginning of our corporate fitness program.

The garage also was the source of rumors in town. Local folk began to whisper that we might be "sneaking in celebrity clients." One person in town started the rumor that he had seen Dolly Parton, Larry Bird, and Paula Abdul enter our garage. We had a lot of fun with this rumor. Later the garage was remodeled to include offices. By 1993 we were completely out of space, with a growing business of nineteen employees.

The hardware store, 142 North Main Street, experience established the foundation for the direction of our company and our commitment to Roanoke. It provided unique office space in a friendly small-town environment conducive to building our business and attracting like-minded employees. There were other important Main Street lessons. Leon Burrey's introduction to Roanoke taught us that necessity is truly the mother of invention. Bob Humphries taught us that it's good to be a good neighbor. Bob Turpin inspired us to be good corporate citizens. Bob Zent taught us to honor and appreciate Roanoke's history. Alice and Rich Pape developed permanent jobs as decorator and contractor, and we learned that the perceived negative of locating in a small town while conducting international business could be—and has been turned into—a distinct advantage in building a successful business.

Our clients in the sports and entertainment industry have seen it all and are not really impressed, I suppose, yet they love visiting us in Roanoke. They find the small town environment an invigorating setting for conducting serious business. They experience small town hospitality in a first-class environment. They realize that we are a company with deep-rooted values and a heart.

In our business, integrity and reliability are essential corporate assets. Employees benefit from Roanoke's quality of life and the opportunity to participate in corporate citizenship. Today, people need more than a job that is just about a paycheck. They want to work for a company in an environment that will enable them to contribute, realize their potential, and help their community. Corporate citizenship is not only good for the community, but is also good for fostering success. And one or more central business enterprises willing to spearhead, and help pay for renaissance in a small town, and who will involve the community as employees, are essential to revitalizing a town.

— *Pete Eshelman*

HISTORY OF 142 NORTH MAIN STREET

The lives and homes of most Roanoke residents have been touched by the rich history that surrounds 142 North Main Street, our hardware store purchase. The current brick building was built in 1905 by Newton Daniel Ellmor Richards, better remembered by his initials, "N. D. E. Richards," or by the more familiar name, "Newt." Richards' father, Daniel, was among the original settlers of the town, arriving in Roanoke in 1851 from Stark County, Ohio. The youngest of ten Richards children, N. D. E. opened Richards Bros. with his brother Marvin in 1889 in a small one-room building located in the middle of the lot where 142 North Main Street now stands. Local legend has it that the brothers took a horse-drawn wagon to Fort Wayne where they bought two hundred dollars' worth of goods from a wholesaler and returned to Roanoke to open their hardware emporium.

The merchandise soon outgrew the store, and a two-story frame building was added on the south side, where the Town Hall is now located. This 1885 structure had a tall wooden façade with "RICHARD BROS. FARM IMPLEMENTS, STOVES AND TINWARE" blazoned across the top. Among the four narrow windows were the words "BUGGIES, WAGONS, HARNESS" while across the entrance was the sign "SHELF HARDWARE." The second floor of this building was used as an opera house and public hall around the turn of the twentieth century.

The current brick building was built next door in 1905, and the frame building became first a storage area and, as times changed, an automobile show room. Richards Bros. sold the Kritt automobile manufactured in Detroit. In 1914, the firm became the agency for Dodge automobiles, and in 1921 a Chevrolet dealership. Marvin Richards sold his interest in the store to his brother in 1916 and N. D. E. Richards' sons joined the operation.

Many residents still recall Ned Richards' Chevrolet dealership on Main Street. The old-fashioned pumps required the user to crank the correct amount of gasoline up into the graded glass container atop the pump before putting the fuel into the automobile. The frame building was torn down in 1946 and replaced by a single-story building serving as an automobile showroom and appliance store. The *Roanoke Review* reported, "the new building greatly improves the appearance of Main Street." Conner Chevrolet

N. D. E. Richards and his children, Ansel Augustus and Gladys Lucille. Richards' wife, Emma Kelsey Richards, died in 1895 and this photo may have been taken about that time.

purchased the building in 1950. It later was renovated for the Town Hall and the permanent home of the Roanoke Town Library.

Richards Bros. Hardware primarily sold farm implements at the outset and slowly expanded to include stoves and tin ware and "shelf hardware." It became the only hardware store in town when Wasmuth & Sons closed in 1920s. Staffed by loyal, knowledgeable employees, the Richards Bros. store became known as a place which stocked just about any hardware item.

Upon the fiftieth anniversary of his business, N. D. E. Richards reflected that his store's success was attributable to its carrying "a complete, diversified, up to the minute line of merchandise." The ultimate critical factor, he said, was to impress both his regular and transient customers that he was fully prepared to meet their needs. Norman Richards remembers his grandfather sitting by the north door to the hardware store, greeting customers—virtually everyone by name—as they entered.

The quality of workmanship in the 1905 brick building is still evident with its carefully preserved tin ceiling and a still functional, hand-operated freight elevator in the rear. A handsome staircase has been added to today's facility in the front to allow access to the second floor. The architectural detail of the exterior—as seen in its decorative brick arches over the windows, for example—is indicative of the period and one reason why the building is a notable example of commercial design of the late nineteenth and early twentieth century.

When examined from the interior, it is obvious that the storage area at the rear of 142 North Main Street was a later addition. At the beginning of the twentieth century, a frame building fronting onto High Street housed Denny Brophy's saloon, one of three in the town. In 1906, the town voted to ban the sale of alcoholic beverages in Roanoke and the saloons were shut down. The structure was torn down and eventually replaced by the Richards' storage area, which opened out from the Main Street building.

The Richards family sold the business to H. L. Bokelkamp in 1950 who, in turn, sold it to Virgil Williams two years later. Like many of its small-town peers, the Roanoke Hardware Store, as it was then known, retained the reputation of being the "go-to place" for its remaining decades, especially when one was looking to repair an older piece of equipment. Regardless of what you needed to repair, it seemed you could walk in and the employees would find it somewhere. And regardless of your experience, you also could get advice on how to make the repairs.

"We had hard-to-find items from earlier eras as well as 'big-ticket' items like Maytag washers and Junger stoves," said Virgil Williams' son, Stephen, an attorney in Fort Wayne who worked in the store as a teenager and young man. The store was open six days a week with evening hours on Friday. "There were not infrequent calls on Sunday when someone's pump broke and they needed a part," Steve Williams recalls. It was a busy store, too, with a good Saturday's receipts totaling a thousand dollars or more in the 1950s.

The store seems more memorable today as one recalls the disappearance of other locally owned, small town hardware stores in the face of corporate competition. The stock spanned the eras of the town, from washboards to washing machines. Steve Williams remembers the second floor with its "not unpleasant" odor of leather from the horse collars, sweat pads, and fly nets, all redolent of a bygone era. Under the eaves of the uppermost parts of the building, the Richardses had hung pelts to cure, and the warm scent of fur was still evident. The hand-operated freight elevator that fascinated a generation of young men before still held its attraction.

The unexpected sudden death of a longtime employee and his own illness prompted Virgil Williams to sell the store to Bob Humphries in 1965, and Bob owned and operated Roanoke Hardware for twenty-five years more. The advent of chain department stores in shopping malls that marketed "handyman" and then "home improvement" merchandise changed the buying habits of the Roanoke community and the nation. Bob Humphries' hardware store closed in 1989 and the building was purchased by American Specialty in 1990.

1992

Roanoke Beautification Project

One building along Main Street had been redone to stand as an example. Clearly, much more remained to be done. My office was a corner office on the second floor, where I spent a lot of time looking out windows, thinking about our business. Sometimes it seems in today's world, where we rely on computers, we don't spend enough time just thinking. It's easy to feel busy when staring at a computer all day. Henry Ford was right when he said "thinking is hard work, and that's why most people don't engage in it." I find it productive to look out windows and think.

Each time I looked out of my office window, I saw buildings in disrepair, ugly streetlights and overhead wires, and crumbling sidewalks. Through the years, because there was no plan or theme for the downtown, each building and business owner treated the buildings as he or she saw fit, which resulted in a hodgepodge of signage and facades typical of most small towns in decline. I knew Roanoke could, and should, look better. This became the inspiration for our commitment to spearheading the downtown beautification plan that would occur two years later.

The rear second floor window was especially interesting. From there I saw a house falling apart at 267 East First Street, on the corner of First and High Streets. This house should have been condemned. Little children living there would play in the yard among the garbage and debris. I felt terrible for those kids living in those conditions. I asked officials whether the house complied with proper codes, and it turned out that the house did not. We contacted the property owner, purchased the property, and the Fire Department helped us demolish the house. We improved the lot for desperately needed parking for our growing company and the Roanoke firefighters.

Roanoke's streets were built for horses and buggies. Our employees were parking on side streets, always searching for available spots. While we converted the eyesore at 267 East First into usable parking, it became the first of five properties we have purchased for current and future parking needs. Our parking lots are landscaped in the downtown beautification theme, and we make them available to the Fire Department and public when needed.

I continued looking out my window on the second floor of the office. I observed those ugly overhead wires and and the rest of the decaying town—definitely the look of yesterday's news. I resolved to do something about it. After all, we had a real estate investment in the downtown and business skills to help develop a plan to improve the downtown area. In addition, having lived in other cities like New Orleans, New York, and Boston, where beautification campaigns had successfully revived business districts and communities, fixing up the downtown seemed like a "no-brainer."

At about the same time, the fledgling Roanoke Chamber of Commerce indicated interest in fixing up the downtown in order to attract new businesses. I was asked by Elsie Wygant and Marilyn Hoy to attend a Chamber meeting to discuss downtown beautification. The Chamber explained their vision for beautification, but they also outlined the reasons such efforts had failed in the past. I offered my ideas, and I was asked if I would head up the committee. My acceptance, I told the Chamber, was conditional on one rule: we would work with a single purpose to make it happen: this would not be an exercise resulting in failure. I had a new business and time was a precious commodity. I didn't particularly like committees because I felt more times than not committees were an inefficient way to achieve goals. To my pleasant surprise, the Chamber agreed. This proved to me that they were serious and committed and with their will, encouraging me to use my business skills, I could lead the way.

The old Chinese proverb that a thousand-mile journey begins with the first step applied. We needed the important first step which was to develop a theme for the beautification. We didn't want a hodgepodge of looks on Main Street. After discussion, we agreed that the beautification theme would reflect Roanoke's turn-of-the-century charm, bridging Roanoke's past to the present.

Another old saying applied: a picture is worth a thousand words. We retained a landscape architect. Kevin McCrory took our ideas and created a draft rendering of what the downtown could look like. We shared this drawing with community leaders, downtown merchants and property owners, and interested citizens. They raised important issues ranging from illumination requirements for streetlights to the actual positioning of trees. We implemented many of these suggestions, and Kevin incorporated them in a final rendering, which reflected the community's vision of what the downtown could look like.

The plan was to beautify the heart of Roanoke's downtown, North Main Street between First and Second streets, with trees, streetlights, and new sidewalks lined with brick, all looking like 1901. A walk down Main Street, we reasoned, would resonate with Roanoke's heritage.

Critics emerged, of course. In small towns one will always find some people afraid of change. Some said they liked the downtown just the way it was. Others said that spending money on beautification was a frivolous exercise when the town was struggling with more important issues. Still others said that the beautification project would be a failure. Beautification had been attempted in the past, but it had failed because it was impossible to get consensus of the downtown business and property owners.

Finally, there was skepticism on financing the project. How much would it cost? Who would pay for it? Who would maintain improvements in the future? At first, because we had put our hearts and souls into developing the plan, the committee members and I took these criticisms personally. But we all sat back and took a deep breath and acknowledged that whenever anyone tries anything positive involving change, it will never be easy. We all needed to keep our focus on the big picture, and view criticisms as constructive challenges, not personal attacks. The committee addressed all the constructive challenges, which strengthened our plan.

Armed with a clear vision, we developed a plan to fund the improvements. There were obstacles: the town of Roanoke had no money available for improvements, and securing grants would take forever. We calculated the cost of the improvements, and we developed a fundraising plan that included sponsorships and donations and participation by property owners. Our sponsorship program paid for the trees, streetlights, and bricks.

An outgrowth of the Beautification Project is the annual Patriotic Pops concert on Main Street, which attracts young and old alike. Some of the young volunteers at the 2002 concert found a moment to pose for a photo.

Here's how it worked: E. J. Richards, a grandson of Roanoke's prominent Richards family, headed the sponsorship effort and was invaluable in selling the trees, streetlights, and bricks. E. J. approached many of the town's longtime residents and families and former business owners with the opportunity to put a family or business name on all of the streetlights and trees, and he was so successful that the bulk of our fund-raising needs were soon met, and the response was so positive that we ran out of trees and streetlights for people to sponsor.

The deep roots and pride that many citizens of Roanoke had in their community and the faith they had in the beautification project expressed their appreciation for the rich quality of life Roanoke had given them. I'm not sure Roanoke is special in this regard; maybe it is, but as a small town the Roanoke experience had positively influenced the lives of many people for many generations, and they rose to appreciate that.

Property owners agreed to pay for the sidewalk improvements in front of their buildings. But how could they fund these capital improvements? Elsie Wygant introduced me to Dave Spangler, president of her bank, the First National Bank of Huntington. Dave was the old-fashioned type of banker who cared about people. He embraced our project, and together we developed an attractive financing program.

Rich Pape of Pape Construction signed on to manage the construction and, once all of the pieces of the plan were in place, the property and business owners signed a petition agreeing to their participation in improving their town's appearance.

August of 1992 was set as a target date to commence construction. I believed firmly in the importance of target dates and timetables for this project. Without target dates to begin and end construction, the project might have languished.

As we progressed with our plan, we kept Town Council members informed and they provided excellent input during the planning stages. Once the plan was completed, it was officially presented to the Town Council and they unanimously approved it and agreed to pave Main Street when construction was completed.

Rich Pape and his crew worked long hours. The electric company removed the ugly overhead streetlights and wires, and to everyone's surprise in town an old brick highway was uncovered under layers of asphalt. As I looked out my second-floor window I could see two narrow indentations in the brick in the middle of the street, which was where wagons and Model Ts once drove through Main Street. One day I hope we can restore the brick streets.

During construction, Main Street was a mess, and some of the merchants who relied on local support saw a temporary decline in their business as people had difficulty entering their stores during construction. However, the enthusiasm for the desperately needed facelift overshadowed this temporary inconvenience. The downtown merchants knew that improving the face of the town would help bring business back to the downtown.

Construction was completed in December 1992, and in July 1993, during a ceremony on Main Street, volunteers, sponsors, donors, merchants, property owners, and town officials who helped make the project a reality were all recognized.

Within three months the downtown went from an eyesore to a source of real pride for those living and working in Roanoke. It gave Roanoke a renewed confidence in itself which stimulated more improvement. When an individual dresses up, he or she feels better, and when a town gets dressed up, it too feels better about itself. When a town feels better about itself, it is capable of doing many positive things.

Since that time, many improvements to building facades have been made. Flowers on Main Street have been added. A landscape company, Changing Seasons, installed hanging flower baskets and flower pots along Main Street. The company's owners Gary Fry, his father, Dale, and mother, Virginia, cared for these flowers as if they were blooming in their own backyard. The Frys became so committed to Roanoke that they moved their landscape and nursery business to the town a few years later.

Each year the flowers have taken on a new level of beauty, which is the result of the Fry's labor of love in caring for Main Street's flowers.

The Taste of Roanoke was Born

Denny Ambriole was the proprietor of Ambriola's Italian restaurant located on the corner of First and Main streets. We had many business dinners at his restaurant, as we talked about the potential for the downtown area. One evening at dinner with Tim, Denny shared with us stories of the great time he'd just had at the Taste of Chicago food festival, showcasing the city's restaurants. Tim and I were familiar with the phenomenon, since we grew up in New Orleans where seafood festivals were a seasonal highlight. I said, "Denny, why don't we start a Roanoke food festival and call it the Taste of Roanoke? Let's close down Main Street and feature your restaurant and the Village Inn." Denny agreed and over dinner that night the "Taste of Roanoke" was born. We assembled a committee with the Chamber of Commerce and held our first Taste of Roanoke in August 1993, featuring Roanoke's restaurants. The community enjoyed it and the Taste of Roanoke has grown into an annual summer family event.

A food festival can draw residents from all over an area to a town undergoing renaissance or wishing to improve itself, providing customers to the local stores and excitement for even more growth.

— Pete Eshelman

1993

First National Bank of Huntington
199 North Main Street

It was time to proceed with the redoing of other key buildings in the town. The First National Bank of Huntington decided to vacate its downtown location and build a new branch office on Highway 24. As a result, the finest example of classic architecture in town was for sale. We had no immediate need for the bank building, but it was obviously worth preserving.

We purchased the bank building and began remodeling it. During one weekend while we were working in the building with Rich and his crew, a man walked into the bank and offered to purchase the old vault doors. His job was to find old banks in Indiana going out of business and purchase the vault doors to be resold to restaurants and/or collectors around the country. His offer for the vaults was almost as much money as we had paid for the entire building. While the price was very tempting, the vaults were part of the history of the bank, and we didn't have the heart to sell them, thinking surely there could be a use for them.

Once we removed the dropped ceiling, we discovered eighteen-foot-high ceilings and beautiful, ornate plaster cornice work. We decided to divide the space in half by creating a second floor that became Tim's apartment. The first floor, which for seventy-five years had been a bank, was donated to the new Roanoke Heritage Center. Bob Zent, E. J. Richards, Bob Hoffman, and other volunteers had recently started the town's Heritage Center and Museum and the space met their immediate needs.

Since that time, the museum has been moved and the old bank space remodeled into the formal dining room for Joseph Decuis, Roanoke's gourmet restaurant. The vaults have been converted into a wine cellar and cigar humidor and the rear room that once housed the town library, a barbershop, and later a law office has been converted into a large temperature-controlled wine room for the restaurant's award-winning collection. Longtime residents of Roanoke who remember the old banking days get pleasure out of visiting the restaurant and seeing the vaults where they once kept their wills and life savings now occupied by fine wines and cigars. Many residents have commented that the current use of the bank is the best use of the building since it was originally built.

— *Pete Eshelman*

HISTORY OF 199 NORTH MAIN STREET

The stately building on the southwest corner of Main and Second streets with its Bedford limestone exterior is more than an outstanding example of Classic Revival architecture. It is a symbol of Roanoke's determination to remain a self-sufficient community in the twentieth century and to be an economically viable town in the twenty-first century.

A humble structure was located on the property soon after the town was established. In the late nineteenth century, in the period of trading success at that time, E. C. Olds is recorded as owning a building on the site that housed Charles Ebersole's boot and shoe store. A series of other shops occupied the building and these were razed when the State Bank of Roanoke's board of directors approved plans in November 1915 for a grand new structure at the site. However, difficulty in securing materials for the interior of the building delayed its completion until 1917.

The town was justifiably proud of the new State Bank of Roanoke building, with its dusky white limestone front and side elevations and marble and mahogany interior. A grand opening was planned, but it was overshadowed by world events. On the day the ceremony was announced, reports emerged from Russia about the overthrow of the tsar. On the eve of the opening, German submarines sank three U.S. vessels, capturing all the front-page headlines. This attack—plus the revelation that Germany was trying to convince Mexico to invade the United States—provoked America to declare war on Germany three weeks later.

In 1919 the directors decided to move the State Bank of Roanoke into the national bank system, bringing what was touted as greater safety and efficiency. In retrospect that sort of financial security was an illusion, since the nation was still without deposit insurance. The newly named First National Bank at Roanoke began operating in August 1919, touting its 150 new safe deposit boxes and state-of-the-art burglar alarm system. The national bank affiliation also brought a change at the helm of the financial institution. D.A. Wasmuth succeeded his father, Augustus, as president, and Augustus became chairman of the board of directors.

World War I left many unsolved problems, as has been shown earlier, in the nation and in Roanoke. It was a time of change, from New York's Wall Street to Roanoke's Main Street. With much of Europe devastated by the war, the United States found itself the most powerful economy in the world.

Built in 1917 to house the State Bank of Roanoke, and now part of the Joseph Decuis restaurant, this striking limestone-faced structure is still an architectural centerpiece on Main Street.

Inflation helped power an upward business cycle that, in turn, fueled a seemingly endless bonanza on Wall Street. The stock market's performance encouraged millions to invest, often at unreasonable margins. At the same time, inflation had its impact in rural America, where farmers and merchants found themselves particularly hard-pressed. For example, E. E. Richards' ledgers for 1923 show it to be another difficult year for his Main Street grocery and dry goods business. The Main Street bank was at the center of these financial challenges.

In 1924 the other bank on Main Street, the Farmer's State Bank, merged with the First National Bank. The Farmer's State Bank had always been smaller than its older competitor and the combined operation, which was located in the First National building, had assets of slightly more than half a million dollars. It seemed like a propitious move. At the First & Farmers, as it was then called, the directors' list read like a Who's Who of Roanoke: D. A. Wasmuth was president and the other members of the board included G. E. Lawrence, three Richards brothers—E. E., N. D. E. and Marvin—Charles C. John, Nathan L. Highlands, E. F. Haines, William Koontz, Lincoln Bolinger, R. H. Tanner, and Harry Dinius. All were prominent and had experience on bank boards.

But they could not anticipate the financial tragedy the nation would face when the "Roaring Twenties" came to an end. The crash of the stock market in October 1929, sent the nation into its worst depression. Still, to many townspeople Wall Street's problems, at first, had little to do with their Main Street bank. There were only scant indications of local problems until President Franklin Delano Roosevelt declared the three-day bank holiday in March 1933 to stop the "run" on banks that was occurring across the nation. More than eleven thousand of the nation's twenty-five thousand banks had gone insolvent in the first three years of the Depression, but few in Roanoke thought that the First & Farmer's might be in trouble, even though the bank's assets had fallen to $265,983 in 1932.

First & Farmer's was among many state-regulated banks that did not pass the solvency test designed by the government. A liquidation order issued October 18, 1933, by the Indiana Department of Financial Institutions declared the bank insolvent, and all its business and property were seized. The eventual payout for depositors in the bank was ten cents on the dollar when the liquidation was completed. Some of today's elderly residents harbor deep resentment at being "robbed" of their savings. One woman recalls a friend telling her to get over to the bank right away and withdraw her money because "something was going to happen." But when the woman asked her employer if she could take a short break to go to the bank and take out her money, he told her she had to stay put while he took care of some business. By the time he returned, the bank was closed. To this day she knows how much money she lost—to the penny.

That oft-heard remark about Roanoke in the Depression, that "times were hard, but we didn't go hungry," was true in part. But farmers particularly were drastically affected by the economic downturn that followed the stock market crash. Low crop prices and shrinking markets caused farmers to cut costs and increase production. "Clean farming"—which called for the elimination of scrub brush and the use of as much of the land as possible—was thought to be the solution, leading to the overproduction of crops. This pushed prices down further. In turn, most farmers refrained from buying nonessentials and this caused merchants to feel the Depression's pinch even more. So while hunger wasn't as widespread in rural Indiana as it was in the cities, the conditions were a recipe for insolvency in much of America's farmland.

The bank's closing shook Roanoke's confidence. It had been able to weather other problems, such as the end of the canal, without such catastrophe. And it would be sixteen years before there would be another bank on Roanoke's Main Street. In the interim, some day-to-day financial functions were provided by businessmen. Alvah L. Blum served as a point of monetary continuity for the town. Blum had been cashier of the bank, and he set up an office in the bank building, providing currency and change and cashing checks for local residents. The safe deposit boxes installed by the Wasmuths remained in operation. Blum, the son of a Roanoke harness maker, was a notary public and provided other recordkeeping services before moving to California in 1948. At that time, he was succeeded by the industrious Joe Merckx, a decorated World War II veteran, who was a multiline insurance agent in town. Merckx was a realtor and a notary public in addition to cashing checks for residents and providing currency and coinage for merchants.

Fortunately, the township was able to buy the building and preserve it. The dream of bringing a bank back to Roanoke never died out, and in 1949 the Roanoke State Bank was brought to fruition through the efforts of men like Harmon Murbach, Jesse Wirts, and Robert Zent.

Murbach had worked at the Department of Financial Institutions and knew he wanted to start a bank. Jesse Wirts, a furniture store owner on Main Street, raised the capital. The bank began with forty thousand dollars in capital—twenty-five thousand in stock; ten thousand surplus; and five thousand undivided profit. Murbach recalled that some of the most unlikely residents became investors. He said that Scott Douglas, who owned the furniture store at Main and First streets and was known for distrusting all banks, told him to come visit before all the stock was subscribed. "Of all people, Scott Douglas gave me five hundred dollars to buy stock in the bank."

Roanoke State Bank's original meeting of stockholders was February 11, 1949, and the bank opened in July, ending a fiscal famine that had extended for sixteen years. The opening was met with great acclaim. The *Roanoke*

Review dedicated ten pages of its July 8 issue to welcoming messages and stories about the opening ceremonies. The building, the newspaper reported, was remodeled to feature an "attractively redecorated banking room" with marble floors and mahogany woodwork.

By December 31, 1949, the bank's assets were $384,995. At the end of 1950, its assets had grown 84 percent to a total of $708,518. It surpassed $1 million in 1952; $2 million in 1960; and $3 million in 1964. When the bank was sold, its 1977 year-end assets were $9.6 million. Demand deposits (checking and savings) exceeded $2.2 million. Despite the growth, the Roanoke State Bank never lost sight of the fact that it was a small-town, Main Street bank. Elsie Wygant, who started working for the bank in 1979 remembers it as a courteous, friendly bank that was very aware of its objectives, which could be found on the back of each quarterly statement: "If you are a customer we thank you for your patronage. If not, we earnestly solicit it."

Looking back, Murbach said the bank was more successful than was expected. Two decades afterward, he is still very proud of the business he helped build and the service the bank offered the community. "It couldn't be done today. A little community like Roanoke could never raise the millions of dollars it would take to start a bank today."

By the late 1970s, computerization was knocking on the door of the Roanoke State Bank. Murbach didn't believe his bank had the capital, or the expertise, to undertake a massive operational changeover, and the Roanoke State Bank was sold to First National Bank of Huntington in April 1978. Over the next two decades, the banking industry went through a wild period of acquisitions and mergers, and the Huntington bank and its Roanoke operation were not exempt from it. In the 1990s it became part of the Fort Wayne National Bank group, only to be acquired by National City Bank of Cleveland In 1998. The building was acquired by American Specialty in 1993 when the bank moved to its new location on First Street at U.S. 24.

The attractive old limestone structure took on a new life.

1994

ANTIQUES MALL
156 NORTH MAIN STREET

By 1994, we had twenty-six employees. Our business had grown significantly with new clients and services.

American Specialty was selected by the Atlanta Committee for the Olympic Games to insure the 1996 Summer Olympic Games in Atlanta. This event was to become the largest peacetime event in the history of the world at that time. American Specialty's selection as provider of insurance for the Olympics enhanced our business reputation around the country and catapulted us to an international platform. It proved that big business can happen in a small town.

We expanded our business with Major League Baseball, inventing an important insurance program that covered the death exposure of players under contract, and we published the first of what is now an annual publication for Major League Baseball, chronicling the trends and costs of injuries in the sport. Tim has since become the industry's leading authority on this subject.

We also expanded our business in amateur sports and developed a program to insure the catastrophic injuries of every NCAA athlete in America.

The Major League Baseball strike temporarily hurt our business and taught us the important lesson of the need for diversification. We began a strategic plan for our products and services following the old farmer's tested philosophy, "Grow different crops because when the corn ain't growin', the wheat will."

This was the period in which we initiated the corporate fitness program in our garage. We purchased our company's first airplane, a Beechcraft Bonanza, to reduce the commute time to connecting airports. This would be the first of seven airplanes that have enabled us to meet our clients' needs and emergencies around the country. Our company was recognized by the Roanoke Chamber of Commerce for the work it had done in spearheading the Roanoke Beautification Project.

Yet, as a growing business, we were again in desperate need of additional office space and parking.

Next door to our office building at 156 North Main Street in another of the old Richards buildings was an antiques mall that was struggling because of lack of retail traffic in the downtown. The owner told us she was closing her business and wondered if we were interested in purchasing the building. The first floor was a large open space, but the second floor was in disrepair with leaking roofs and crumbling plaster.

We purchased the building and converted it into offices that currently accommodate twenty-three employees and our boardroom. The entrance to the antiques mall became our main lobby entrance.

— Pete Eshelman

★

HISTORY OF 156 NORTH MAIN STREET

The handsome row of brick buildings on North Main Street that constitute the primary part of the American Specialty office complex is attributable to one man who had a vision not only for his business, but also for his community.

Ervin E. Richards. who was a central force in the town's development for half a century, came to Roanoke at age fourteen in 1873 to be a clerk and worked in Dr. C. L. Richart's drugstore on Commercial Row, now known as High Street. In 1884 he bought a grocery business, built a two-story brick building on Main Street and partnered with William L. Zent. A photograph from1888 shows them proudly standing in front of their store, two successful-looking young merchants. In a year Zent would depart and Richards would operate his growing business alone until 1910 when his eldest son, Donald E., joined the firm. Two more sons would join the firm and E. E. Richards & Sons would grow into a very prominent Roanoke institution.

In July 1898 Richards announced he would demolish the frame structures from his building to the Charles Koontz's bakery (next to John Hackett & Son's drugstore on the corner) and replace them with a single-story brick building row of stores. He revised his plans a month later to make them all two stories. They are typical of commercial structures of the Victorian era, with a distinctive limestone lintel over the windows. One doorway still has the cast-iron posts from the Bass Foundry in Fort Wayne. Popular in the urban areas as early as the 1850s, cast-iron components gained acceptance in rural small towns as the Victorian style architecture became dominant.

Although it is difficult to see at first glance, 156 North Main Street, the central building of our headquarters, was not part of that reconstruction. While the visual effect of the exterior is that of a single, consistent row of

The start of the fifty-three-year career of E. E. Richards (in front of doorway) as a Roanoke businessman began with this small store on Main Street and with a partner, William Zent (right). This would grow into E. E. Richards & Sons—and later Richards Department Store.

buildings, the structure at 156 North Main is a story taller than the others and the brick is a slightly different hue. In 1898, the site was vacant. Even when the rest of the Richards buildings were completed, this parcel remained empty except for a wooden outside stairway leading to the second story over Richards' store.

Among the earliest reminiscences of the town was that there was a small brown house on the site, set well back from the street. This would have been in the 1850s or 1860s, when Main Street was not Roanoke's main street. The house was demolished in the 1870s or 1880s as the town's economic activity moved away from the Wabash & Erie Canal.

The current building owes its existence directly to the small neon-accented second-story sign that is perpendicular to the street: The square and compass of the Masons and the star of its women's counterpart, the Order of the Eastern Star. Among the oldest in Indiana, Roanoke's Masonic Lodge was formed in November 1855, meeting initially in a small room in a building overlooking the canal. It became an official part of the charitable, benevolent, educational and religious society of Freemasonry in May 1856. Its members included such leaders as Dr. C. L. Richart, Samuel H. Zent, and William Hendry and by 1870 the active membership exceeded one hundred men. In 1874 a fire destroyed its first meeting place along with the records of the lodge. A lodge hall was erected in 1883 and, while considered "commodious," the membership outgrew it. The need for a new, permanent home became increasingly pressing by the Roanoke Chapter, Order of the Eastern Star, being granted a charter in April 1887. An agreement was reached with E. E. Richards in 1914 to construct a building that would be used for mercantile and Masonic purposes on the first and second floors, respectively. The Masonic Lodge was given a "perpetual easement" for its quarters. The building was finished in the winter and the new Masonic hall dedicated in February 1915. The *Huntington Herald* reported that the Masonic hall consisted of three principal rooms along with a reception area, property room, and a well-equipped kitchen. The main rooms had indirect lighting, dark mahogany woodwork, and beamed ceilings. The toastmaster for the dedication was E. M. Wasmuth, son of the pioneer businessman Augustus Wasmuth. Both of the Wasmuths as well as E. E. Richards were members of the lodge.

The building at 156 North Main Street housed the dry goods portion of the E. E. Richards & Sons store for almost fifty years, even after its namesake had died and his sons had sold it to another merchant. The name E. E. Richards was synonymous with caring service and commitment. Richards took great pride with being a household name in the area and with the claim that his combined stores in a row on North Main were "the largest small-town department store in Indiana."

The attention E. E. Richards paid to detail and to knowing his customers is still evident today in his ledgers and journals. Richards kept meticulous records, so he knew what his customers bought and what they might be interested in. For example, an entry from the first month of his store's operation notes that Mr. and Mrs. J. W. Parks were just married and lists their purchases and sizes.

But E. E. Richards was more than a successful businessman; he was a successful citizen, too. Richards was not satisfied with just improving the business façade of North Main Street. He was a member of the town board and struggled with them to improve Roanoke. He detested the wooden sidewalks, their unattractive appearance, their need for repair and the danger they represented to people using them. He disliked the dirt streets that were either mud-clogged or dust-filled. When the council wouldn't approve new sidewalks, Richards enlisted other merchants and the Methodist Episcopal Church to pay for the laying of concrete sidewalks in the town. He was a champion of bricking Main Street and Second Street and was instrumental in the town's putting in its first sewer.

While he had foresight for his community, Richards was still a man of his own times. He was careful and considerate. In his January 1920 advertisement for the store's semiannual sale, Richards notes: "Unusual bargains at profitable savings. We do not advocate overbuying, but we do advise economy in buying." Among the items listed were: ladies shoes, grey and field-mouse high top and high heel, regular $10, sale price $7.75; and leatherette coat for the man that drives the car, regular $19.50, sale price $16. For more than the obvious reason, it was a different time.

When E. E. Richards died in 1937, his sons Donald and Noel operated the store. Donald Richards began in the men's portion of the store and then moved to the grocery, while Noel Richards spent his career with the men's department. The second son, Eldon, was the business's bookkeeper. The dry goods store at 156 North Main Street was sold in 1948 to Carl Schafer, who had worked for the famed Wolf & Dessauer's department store in Fort Wayne. The building was remodeled after Richards closed, for a time serving as a drugstore before being sold to Sharon Stultz for the unusually named Antiques & Not Mall, which was closed at the end of 1993.

For small-town restorations, the principle involved in the redo of 156 and contiguous buildings here is that renovation and redesign of *several* buildings must be undertaken. Renaissance happens over several years and with consistent refurbishing and continuous town revitalization. It can't stop after only one or two buildings.

★ ★ ★ ★

1995

ODD FELLOWS LODGE
141 NORTH MAIN STREET

Across the street from my office was the Odd Fellows building. The second floor housed the lodge, and the first floor was occupied by a video store and hairdresser's salon. John Klaehn, one of the members of the Odd Fellows lodge, told me he was afraid they would have to sell the building. The lodge's membership was declining because its members were aging, many of them having difficulty climbing the steep stairs to the second floor. He asked if we were interested in purchasing the building.

During a tour of the second floor of 141, Klaehn confided to me that the lodge would like to stay in Roanoke, because it had been located in the town for more than fifty years. That night at dinner, Tim and I came up with an idea. The next day we made an offer to purchase the building, giving the Odd Fellows a fifteen-year lease on the first floor, and replacing the video store, which was going out of business.

Klaehn presented our proposal to the lodge, which enthusiastically accepted it, since it solved their needs: first-floor space, ability to stay in Roanoke, and the freeing up of their capital for other uses. Rich Pape completed the renovation construction for the lodge and for Terri Taylor's beauty salon on the first floor.

American Specialty converted the second floor into a corporate fitness center. Fitness had become an important part of the American Specialty culture. Our business requires long hours, high stress, and a lot of travel. If an employee is not physically fit, he or she cannot handle the pace of the business. Also, I believe one thinks better if he or she is fit, and this can be a corporate advantage. We retained the services of a personal trainer, Gregg Graham, who has structured the fitness program around resistance and aerobics training. Today, Valerie Powers acts as fitness director, and more than half of our "corporate athletes" participate regularly in the fitness program.

— *Pete Eshelman*

★

HISTORY OF 141 NORTH MAIN STREET

On the central medallion of the parapet of this building is chiseled the letters IOOF, a reference to an almost forgotten part of the history of Middle America and Roanoke. The abbreviation stands for the Independent Order of Odd Fellows, one of the oldest fraternal orders in the United States, with its inception in Baltimore being in 1819. It was part of a movement that began in England in the 1700s, when was considered odd to find people organized for the purpose of giving to those in need and of pursuing projects for the benefit of all mankind. To this day, the organization aspires to its original mission, for example, to "visit the sick, relieve the distressed, bury the dead and educate the orphan." Odd Fellows was the first national fraternity to include both men and women.

The Little River Lodge No. 275 was granted its charter in 1867 with five members. Its first official meeting facility was the second floor of a frame building on Second Street, which was built in 1870. This lodge was described as having the "neatest and most tastefully furnished lodge halls in northern Indiana" at the time. It was used for fifty-three years for Odd Fellows' functions until the new building was erected on Main Street. The Second Street building burned in the late 1930s and was replaced by Hartley's Garage.

In 1883 the lodge purchased ten acres on the north side of town as a cemetery, which is now known as Glenwood Cemetery.

The commercial style structure on North Main Street, with its two large-windowed stores on the first floor, housed many retail businesses over the past eighty years in addition to Odd Fellows and Rebekah functions on the second floor. While furniture-store owner Scott Douglas was the first tenant with a showroom, the chief occupant for many years was Jennings Electrical Store, selling International Harvester freezers and refrigerators, among other

The Odd Fellows lodge was very active in Roanoke after its creation in the mid-nineteenth century.

appliances. The post office operated from 141 North Main Street for many years. In addition, there have been groceries, electrical stores, and beauty salons located there. The Odd Fellows and Rebekahs flourished for many years and held a gala mortgage burning ceremony in November 1946. The organization's numbers decreased during the last half of the twentieth century, forcing it to put the building up for sale. The Odd Fellows closed the Little River Lodge and merged with Fort Wayne in the early 1980s because there were too few remaining members in Roanoke.

It became one of the central core of restoration which constituted the growing renaissance of the town—approaching a critical mass.

★ ★ ★ ★

1996

Condemned Home, 208 Vine Street
Winans Insurance, 196 North Main Street
Greg's Market, 164 North Main Street
NAPA Auto Parts, 191 North Main Street

To say that 1996 was a busy and challenging year is an understatement. We continued to experience significant growth in our insurance business and our newly formed consulting operations. Further, it was the year we were greatly tested.

In 1996, we insured the Atlanta Summer Olympic Games, which proved to be a very complex task. No books existed from which to draw experience and information. In fact, we were helping write the book. Along with the Organizing Committee's management and insurance representatives, we worked with Fireman's Fund Insurance Company to uniquely design coverages and risk management services. In our business, the intangible product called insurance becomes tangible when a claim occurs and the insurance is called on to respond.

The July 27 bombing at Centennial Park was a tragedy that sparked international concern and sympathy. It resulted in two deaths and injuries to 110 innocent people who were enjoying the Olympic experience in the park. We successfully responded to the organizing committee's needs, proving that American Specialty was cool under fire and delivered on its promises when the going got tough.

It was a busy time for our rapidly growing business in other ways. We purchased five more properties in downtown Roanoke; truly reinforcing that critical mass that was defining the restored town.

208 Vine Street

Highly visible as you entered Roanoke was a home in disrepair at 208 Vine Street. It gave the wrong impression about the town's condition, particularly to those first-time visitors driving in from the Fort Wayne airport. The county was going to condemn it, and so I contacted the owner and found that she was an elderly lady who neither had the financial means to improve the building to the county's specifications, nor did she understand the legal issues about to confront her. I told her that we would be willing to buy the house and raze it to create a greenbelt entrance into Roanoke. She was relieved and sold the property. We subsequently demolished the building, and landscaped the property, thus creating a pleasant entrance into the town.

196 NORTH MAIN STREET

Marlin Winans, the proprietor of Winans Insurance Agency, was moving his business closer to Fort Wayne. The days of the small town insurance agency were numbered, and Marlin did not have sufficient business to justify an office in Roanoke.

He approached me and asked if we were interested in purchasing his building, where the first floor housed insurance offices, and the second floor was an apartment. We had no immediate use for the building, but did have a growing need to provide some form of accommodations for out-of-town clients visiting our company. We purchased the building, and gutted the first and second floors. We converted the second floor into our Hall of Fame Suites, which include the American League Suite and the National League Suite. These accommodations have been used for clients who visit us or employees who are moving to the area and need temporary housing.

As we were under construction, my good friend Eugene Parker, a sports agent practicing in Fort Wayne, told me he was looking for office space away from the downtown Fort Wayne traffic. I told him I had the perfect solution for him: "Roanoke!" He didn't know of its existence. I told him how we enjoyed this small town and suggested headquartering his sports agency on Main Street would be good for his business, just as it had been for ours. Feeling a little like Leon Burrey trying to recruit us to move to Roanoke, I told him the rent would be reasonable and we would build him first-class office space. I think "reasonable rent" got his attention. Eugene moved his company to Roanoke and has since built one of the top sports management companies in the United States. His story is truly an American success story developed through serving others.

— *Pete Eshelman*

HISTORY OF 196 NORTH MAIN STREET

The structure on the southeast corner of North Main and Second streets was by almost universal acclaim in Roanoke "the center of town" for much of the twentieth century. The site of a series of drugstores, it is the subject of fond memories for most people who grew up in the town.

The building was the site of the "Old Reliable Drug Store" by the start of the century, run by John Hackett, one of Roanoke's pioneer businessmen. One of the town's most influential citizens, Hackett went to work in R. C. Ebersole's drugstore in 1857. After the Civil War, as the mercantile era flourished in Roanoke, he held a series of jobs before joining James B. Slusser in a grocery-store partnership. Gradually, the store added a large stock of medicines and Slusser exited. Hackett's store moved to this site and his son, Charles L. Hackett, joined him before he retired in 1912 from what was then known as "Old Reliable Drug Store." The younger Hackett died in 1918 and the store was acquired by Harry Purvis, who operated a pharmacy there in the 1920s, with the building sporting a large sign reading "PURVIS MEANS PURE DRUGS."

Purvis sold the business to his brother-in law, Charles Stabler in 1923, and it was as Stabler's Drug Store that it realized its heyday. Generations of young people experimented with different flavored Coca-Colas or phosphates at the Stabler's fountain as they munched Seyfert's potato chips. The newsstand was on the right as a customer entered, filled with magazines like *True Story*, which one former resident noted were "pre-read by the help." The store featured the patent medicines of the era as well as mascara, nail polish, and hair curlers.

Yet, like many other individual pharmacies, the Roanoke drugstore couldn't compete with large chains. The building was sold to Marlin Winans, who operated an insurance agency there before consolidating the operation into one at Time Corners. It was sold to American Specialty in early 1996.

Today, in comparison to the days when town activity focused on the drugstore, there is little local attention paid to the business on the corner; however, it is well known in the professional sports industry around the country. As has been said, Maximum Sports Management was begun in 1978 by Eugene Parker and now represents some of the top professional football players in the United States. Among his clients are National Football League stars Emmitt Smith, Curtis Martin, and Rod Woodson.

John Hackett went to work in a drugstore before the Civil War and operated this store until 1912. The building was a focal point for the community as it housed both Purvis and Stabler's drugstores until the 1970s.

Parker, whose hometown is Fort Wayne, was an outstanding basketball player himself. His career included four years as a starter on the Purdue University basketball team and induction into the Indiana Basketball Hall of Fame. Parker was drafted by the San Antonio Spurs of the National Basketball Association in 1978. But Parker gave up sports to practice law and entered into the sports representation field when he agreed to help his friend and Purdue teammate Roosevelt Barnes negotiate a contract with the Detroit Lions.

Maximum Sports Management—which is now part of Assante Corporation's sports management division—is located here, far from the bright lights of New York and Los Angeles, because Parker feels it demonstrates his values to his clients. "They see that I'm not in the business for the glamour, but to serve their interests in the best way possible. Being from the Midwest signifies a certain work ethic and our clients feel comfortable with that. They know they can rely on us and trust us."

His philosophy and personality well suit the town's flavor and new purpose.

★

164 NORTH MAIN STREET

Adjacent to the Antiques Mall which the company had purchased for office expansion was 164 North Main Street. The building, owned by an individual who had purchased it as an investment, housed Greg's Market on the first floor and rental apartments on the second floor. We purchased the building and began the process of dealing with the tenants.

Greg was struggling to run a grocery business on Main Street. A strong individual, Greg was under-capitalized and constantly low on inventory, but he would not give up. Now he was faced with competition, as Mike Rogers opened Hoosier Foods around the corner, at High and First streets. Mike, whose family had been the leading grocer in the Fort Wayne area for six decades, was attracted to Roanoke by the town's beautification efforts and was confident that it would inspire future growth. The Rogers family had developed a business model providing small grocery stores for small towns underserved by the national chains, and Mike chose Roanoke to put the concept into action.

We desperately needed additional office space, and Greg's Market was our natural course of expansion. I asked Greg if he would be willing to relocate his business. At first, he was very reluctant. I told him that as a friend and outside observer, I thought he would have a difficult time surviving. He said he would think about it, and we would talk the next day. When we met, I fully expected him to be upset with me for suggesting he close his business down, but to my surprise he thanked me and said that I made him realize that he was failing and he was afraid to give up. He had decided to

The Heroes

Townspeople who have served valiantly in the nation's armed forces are considerably more in number than one would imagine. For example, considering its population in the 1860 census, Roanoke had a sizable representation in the Union Army. Among them was William McGinnis, who enlisted as a first lieutenant of Company H, 75th Regiment, Indiana Infantry in August 1862, in whose memory the town's Grand Army of the Republic (GAR) chapter was named.

McGinnis was not your typical young soldier. He was forty-five years old and had five children ranging in age from two to twelve years old. Listed as a mechanic in civilian life, McGinnis was mustered into the Army as a captain in January 1863 under Colonel J. J. Robinson. The Indiana 75th fought at Perryville, Kentucky, in 1862 and Chickamauga and Chattanooga in 1863 before becoming part of Sherman's army in the Georgia-Carolinas campaign that ended the war in 1865.

Records show McGinnis had been hospitalized for an illness in August 1863 in Nashville, Tenn. He was wounded on September 20, 1863, at the Battle of Chickamaugua—where more Hoosier soldiers died than at any other Civil War battle—and taken prisoner. McGinnis died at Libby Prison, Savannah, Georgia, on August 31, 1864.

Augustus Wasmuth was more typical of the Union soldier, enlisting at the age of twenty-one with the 47th Regiment, Indiana Infantry in 1862. Most of the men of his company, as was practice of the time, came from Huntington, North Manchester, Roanoke and Bluffton. Wasmuth and the rest of Company E served with General U. S. Grant's forces in the campaign to capture Vicksburg, Mississippi. At Champion Hill, the bloodiest battle of the campaign, the 47th Indiana suffered 143 killed and wounded. Six men of Company E—including Private William Hackett of Roanoke—were killed in the May 16, 1863, battle while two more men died from wounds received in that battle. The regiment was then sent with General Nathaniel Banks to Mobile for the unsuccessful Red River Campaign. Other engagements in which they fought along the Mississippi River included the assault and capture of Memphis, where Wasmuth was among the first to land.

Private Hackett was not the only casualty from Roanoke. Four other men who were among the original enlistees with Company E died in the war either from wounds or disease, among them Eli Dinius, killed at Jackson, Mississippi, on July 12, 1863. Eight more recruits, who joined in January or March 1864, died in service that year.

The lives of many men were changed dramatically by the events of the war, for both good and bad. Benjamin Payton of Roanoke joined Company E in December 1861. He was promoted to second lieutenant on March 1, 1864, to first lieutenant on January 1, 1865, and to captain on March 1, 1865. He mustered out with the regiment on October 23, 1865.

Two other Roanoke men must have held strong

A gathering of Civil War veterans from the Roanoke area posed for this early 1900s photo of the William McGinnis chapter of the Grand Army of the Republic.

abolitionist beliefs because records indicate they transferred to the 33rd U.S. Colored Troops Regiment. Jacob W. Hart and Harry W. Zents, both of whom enlisted in December 1861 in Company E, received promotions to first lieutenant to the regiment that had been organized as the 1st South Carolina Volunteer Infantry, Colored. It was redesignated the 33rd Regiment in February 1864 and was engaged in the Battle of Honey Hill, South Carolina, a disaster for federal forces.

Apparently, Company E came into contact with African-American soldiers during its September 1863 campaign in Brashear City (now Morgan City), Louisiana. Wasmuth wrote to his wife-to-be that "we had two or three (regiments) of colored troops with us and they were good soldiers and seemed to be proud of their position."

More than one hundred men and three women from Roanoke answered their nation's call-to-arms for World War I. Two died in the course of the war, and in 1928 they were honored on Decoration Day with the dedication of a small drinking fountain on Second Street, just off North Main Street. Hundreds of people crowded into the intersection for the ceremony that honored Private Robert Mayne, who was just twenty-one years old when he was killed in the Argonne battle line near St. Juvin, France, on November 1, 1918, and nurse Grace Buell, who was twenty-three when she died on October 18, 1918, at an Army base hospital at Portsmouth, England. Their deaths, according to Irene Simonds Richards, who presented the dedication speech, "shocked the community, for both had grown up here, walked these streets, graduated from our high school, and from its doors had gone out to useful occupations. Their pure, clean, happy lives honored their families, the school, and the community."

Above the distinctive fountain, which was sponsored by the Roanoke Library Club, rose a large pillar, and atop it stood a sculpture of a great, flying golden eagle. Over the years, the fountain was vandalized many times. Local lore has it that someone destroyed the original eagle by detonating a firecracker in its beak.

Today, the American Legion has restored the fountain with a small plaque and a brick column with a small eagle atop. Still, it is a far cry from the hopes of its originators who dreamed that "as people refresh themselves from its cooling waters, they will happily remember these two and the splendid service they gave and the sacrifice they made that we might live better and happier lives."

Three servicemen from World War II have been recently honored as part of Roanoke's Patriotic Pops celebrations. Sergeant Harold J. Amstutz entered military service in the summer of 1941 and was stationed in Great Britain. His service included five major battles in Belgium and Germany, including the Battle of the Bulge. He was cited for courage and coolness under fire and earned two Bronze Stars.

The war had a series of terrible ironic twists for Joseph Merckx who was thirty-three years old and the father of three daughters when he was drafted into the Army. Merckx was born in Belgium and smuggled out of the country during World War I when the Germans occupied that nation. In the Second World War, Merckx fought in the European Theatre of Operations and participated in the capture of the French town of Verdun, near the Belgian border. Merckx went on to fight in the most desperate moment for the Allies after D-Day—the Battle of the Bulge. He guided replacements to the front line and brought wounded soldiers to the rear. After three months of being under enemy fire, Merckx and others were ordered to England for rest. But the ironic twists were not done: The plane taking the men to safety lost its radio and was downed by friendly fire near Rouen. Despite suffering a severe back injury, Merckx managed to pull the other troops from the wreckage.

In 2002 Ralph W. Hine was living with his wife within a mile of where his grandfather had lived in the early days of town. It was hard to imagine that this quiet, unassuming man in his nineties had been part of the Army's most daring invasions, earning the Bronze Star and two Purple Hearts.

Hine was thirty-three years old when he was drafted into the army in 1942 and was assigned after basic training to the 82nd Airborne Division. At the time, the army had decided to experiment with gliders to carry troops and equipment into combat along with a parachute assault. Hine's job was to pack his Jeep and anti-tank assault weapon into a glider which, after it had been towed near the target by a C-47 transport, would be piloted into a combat landing area. Glider assaults were risky ventures since the planes were slow, had little armor and landings were little more than controlled crashes. Hine participated in the North African invasion at Tunis and the parachute/glider assault into Sicily and Salerno in 1943. But these proved to be but mild rehearsals for the largest airborne assault in history, the invasion of France on June 6, 1944. The night before, three parachute regiments and reinforced glider infantry took off from England for a destination behind enemy lines in an effort to keep Nazi reinforcements from reaching the coastal invasion. Fewer than half the gliders in the Normandy invasion reached their landing zones. The others, lodged in hedgerows, struck German obstructions or floundered in flooded lowlands. The U.S. troops were scattered and Hine was looking for his unit when an officer said, "I suppose you're looking for your buddies, but there are twenty some German tanks we're looking for." The officer, it turned out, was Major General Matthew B. Ridgeway, commander of the 82nd who had jumped with his men and led the fight to secure Sainte-Mère-Église and cut off enemy communications to Cherbourg.

For thirty-three days without relief or replacements, the 82nd fought the German army. Before they were pulled back for refitting, a total of 5,245 paratroopers were killed, wounded, or listed as missing. A month later the 82nd spearheaded a "leap-frog" assault beyond the Rhine, behind German lines, to seize key roads and bridges. On September 20, Hine's division was the only one in Beek, Holland, and was instructed to take the city. The Germans were waiting for them. After the initial assault, Hine had to remove his Jeep from the town because of heavy enemy shelling. Although he had been wounded slightly, Hine then volunteered to drive a

medical officer back into Beek where he helped pull the wounded from the town as the enemy was reentering. He went back into Beek a third time to reposition an antitank gun so it could deliver more effective fire. In the end, the paratroopers prevailed and for his heroic conduct Hine was awarded a Bronze Star by Major General James N. Gavin.

There were men who served in the Korean Conflict and the Vietnam War. The latter claimed the lives of two young Roanoke men. Marine Corps Lance Corporal Terry Gene Graft was nineteen years old when he was mortally wounded by enemy artillery fire in the province of Quang Tri, South Vietnam, on August 31, 1969. Marine Corps Lance Corporal Thomas Duane Worrel was mortally wounded by enemy small-arms fire on April 23, 1970, in the province of Quang Nam, South Vietnam. He was twenty years old.

Testing the "cooling waters" of the Memorial Fountain was the climax of the dedication ceremony on Decoration Day in 1928.

close his business and wanted us to give him enough time to vacate the premises. When Greg closed his business, we began construction on additional office space.

When the second-floor tenants left, the second floor was gutted and converted into office space, which currently houses our executive offices and finance department.

One of the effects of small-town revitalization is that it helps residents who may be stuck in old patterns to reassess and move forward. Thus revitalization has personal elements too.

— *Pete Eshelman*

★

HISTORY OF 164 NORTH MAIN STREET

One pivotal measure of a small town's self-sufficiency is whether it has a grocery store. From the earliest days of settlement to today's cosmopolitan lifestyle, the existence of a grocery is the mark of viability for the community. There were several grocers in Roanoke's history before E. E. Richards purchased the stock from his employer, J. M. Slusser, in 1884, but none were as long-lasting and few as popular. Richards, and later his sons, demonstrated that Roanoke warranted, and could support, a sizable grocery.

The store's history is a good example of the changes in small business. When he completed the entire string of buildings on North Main Street, Richards did not occupy all of them at once. Instead, he rented the storefronts he could not afford to immediately occupy. For example, Evan Bell celebrated Christmas week in 1898 by opening his "elegant meat market" in one of Richards' buildings, and a photograph from early 1899 shows a lunch room in another building. Later, Bell took on Henry Kress as a partner

E. E. Richards' grocery in the 1920s. From left: Raymond Kime, E. E. Richards, George Slaker, Noel Young, Velma Runyan, Ruth Cramer, and Helen Zent.

and they moved their operation into the next Richards' store. Eventually, E. E. Richards was operating in all of his buildings.

When he began his grocery operation, E. E. Richards patronized local producers when he could. This he did not do in his dry goods business which prided itself in offering top-of-the-line products from mercantile centers like Chicago, St. Louis, and New York. Richards' grocery store records show he bought bread from Fred Goodwald's bakery on Main Street and dairy products from the Roanoke Creamery. There was a margarine product purchased from Miami Butterine Company, and eggs were from the Indiana Hatchery. Flour came from the mills in the town. All of the produce wholesalers in the early 1920s' ledgers seemed to be Fort Wayne businesses. This, of course, was indicative of a time when refrigerated transportation was unavailable and most food items did not include preservatives.

The store was known for its customer service. "Mother would call down and ask for fifty-cents of Swiss steak and then say, 'And please make sure it's enough to feed us all.' They knew each customer and each family," Phyllis Witherow remembered.

However, neither E. E. Richards nor his sons were wedded to the past. During World War II, Donald Richards installed Gibson slant-front refrigerated meat cases to make product more visible to the customer. When James Brouwer bought the store and renamed it the Roanoke Super-Market after the war, he put in individual meat lockers for customers. These heavily insulated two-by-two-foot storage units enabled consumers to buy a side of beef at a favorable price, then have it cut up and stored at the market for use when they needed it.

Bob Turpin opened his store in 1982 and operated it for a decade, growing the operation from less than four thousand square feet to ten thousand square feet. It was a full-service market featuring fresh-cut steaks, chicken and chops, and fresh produce, open every day until 9 P.M. But Turpin watched in dismay as one Main Street store after another closed, victims of the larger malls, and finally realized the facility would not always be a grocery store.

191 North Main Street

When we first moved to town, this nondescript building housed the Cornerstone Alliance Church. Before we even knew the church had moved to its new building, NAPA Auto Parts had moved in with its trademark bright yellow and blue colors on Main Street. The store did not fit into the downtown beautification theme and was a classic case of the town's lacking ordinances governing exterior aesthetics. The NAPA store closed within a short period of time because of little traffic and the lack of parking on Main Street.

The owner approached me and asked if American Specialty was interested in purchasing his building. It was a great opportunity to bring the structure back to the beautification theme, and we purchased the building.

Because our business had grown and more and more people from around the world were visiting our offices, we wanted a private dining facility to accommodate business meetings. We hired Lisa Williams as our corporate chef in 1997 and converted the first floor of the old Roanoke State Bank building into an executive dining room, moving the Heritage Center, which had occupied the space, to the remodeled space in the old NAPA building and creating another continuum of restored, beautiful buildings across the street from corporate headquarters.

— Pete Eshelman

History of 191 North Main Street

The property alongside the former First National Bank, now part of the new restaurant complex, has been the site of a range of commercial operations far less elegant than a gourmet restaurant. The original building on the site was constructed during or just after the Civil War by a Mr. Duck who had entered into partnership with A. P. Koontz in the building of furniture and coffins. The front room of the building displayed their handmade tables, dry sinks and bureaus, and cushioned final resting places for Roanoke's departed, while the back room was used as a workshop. Mr. Duck's first name is unknown since he sold his interest in the stock and the building and moved out of town. In 1921 Dr. Sylvanus Koontz termed the structure "a relic of antiquity," and noted that "this old and dilapidated building adds but little grace and beauty to the fine structure at its side on the north." In the 1920s the building was used as a vulcanizing plant before burning down.

In the 1940s, photographs of the site show a large display board with the names of all Roanoke's soldiers in World War II. Residents can't say when or why it disappeared, and Harmon Murbach, who built the current structure, doesn't recall it being there when construction started. Murbach said he built the building for George McPherren, who opened the Roanoke Pastry Shop, featuring breads, cakes, and cookies. McPherren, brother of longtime educator William McPherren, had experience as a baker and wanted his own place. The shop grew, and in 1951, for twenty-five cents you could enjoy a ham salad sandwich made with bread from the bakery.

The building also housed the Crestwoods Village Shop, a frame shop and gallery established by Mildred Hendricks. The shop moved two doors down to 159 North Main in the 1970s where it is now owned and operated by Wally Orr. The NAPA store was the final tenant before the building was acquired by American Specialty.

★ ★ ★ ★

1997

ROANOKE'S PATRIOTIC POPS CONCERT
VACANT PROPERTY, 148 HIGH STREET

Roanoke's downtown had been the heart of commerce and entertainment for the community for more than 125 years. Commerce had declined, yet with Main Street now renovated, the area seemed again to be the perfect setting for community entertainment. The main block between First and Second streets could be easily closed from traffic, creating an intimate setting.

The Taste of Roanoke had proven that this setting was distinctive. While the community had many events during the course of the year—Christmas in the Village, Springtime in the Village, and Fall Festival—it seemed logical to create a world-class entertainment event that would bring recognition to the town and raise money for future beautification projects.

One Sunday morning, Alice and I were watering flowers on Main Street. Someone could have fired a cannon down the street without hitting anything, with not a car or person in sight. Looking down that row of renovated buildings with the beauty of new lampposts and flowers, we saw the positive effects of the beautification. Now Main Street seemed to long for a spectacular special event for the community. On the spur of the moment, I told Alice, "I think we ought to stage a Patriotic Pops Concert on Main Street with an orchestra. Can you imagine patriotic music and a thousand people watching in this setting?" Somewhat to my surprise she agreed, although she was a bit skeptical. We had experienced what a wonderful patriotic event could do to inspire a town. While living in Boston both of us enjoyed the Fourth of July Concerts on the Esplanade on the Charles River in Boston, listening to Arthur Fiedler and the Boston Pops Orchestra. We were two people of a hundred thousand enjoying a spectacular and moving event. I presented the idea to the Beautification Committee and they agreed it would be a great idea. We developed a business plan, contacted the Fort Wayne Philharmonic, which coincidentally was beginning a summer pops concert series, and obtained the permission from the town of Roanoke to block off the street. We held the inaugural Patriotic Pops Concert on July 3, 1997.

Some people in town thought we were crazy. No one would listen to classical music in Roanoke! Others thought we could never raise the money to pay the orchestra—in excess of seventeen thousand dollars—let alone cover all the expenses and make a profit for the beautification program. Nevertheless, American Specialty assumed the role of managing sponsor, responsible for organizing the event with company volunteers and for raising money to cover all bills. We agreed to donate all profits, if any, to the Roanoke Beautification Foundation. As our chief fund-raiser, Alice developed a plan for sponsorships, and others in the company helped in the various capacities, such as parking, security, ticket sales, and accounting. Each year, the number of volunteers has grown.

The night before the first concert we all had the jitters. Alice had been successful in securing sponsors' contributions to cover the expenses, so the real sense of accomplishment would be seeing a sold-out house of a thousand people watching the Philharmonic under starlit summer skies. In the middle of the night I woke up from a dream in which everything was set up but there were only two people in the audience.

The concert was a spectacular success: a perfect night with a full house, great patriotic music, and a unique opportunity for the community to be together in a positive experience celebrating our country's freedom and Roanoke's revival of Main Street. The concert has become an annual tradition.

In 2001, we added a special feature, honoring Roanoke residents who have served our country. Roanoke resident Colonel Perry Collins of the Air National Guard at Fort Wayne has managed this aspect of the program each year. It is great for neighbors and children to learn about the sacrifices some of their neighbors have made in defending our country's freedom.

The concert has evolved from a community entertainment event into an important lesson about patriotism and freedom.

Those contemplating small-town revival need to look closely at meaningful entertainment spectaculars to draw people into the exciting, newly revitalized community.

148 High Street

The Whistle Stop pizza shop owned a vacant lot adjacent to our company parking lot at 148 High Street. We purchased the property from Ellis and Pat Line and converted it into desperately needed parking for our growing company.

— *Pete Eshelman*

History of High Street's Business Area

It is difficult to envision today, but High Street was busier than Main Street during Roanoke's canal era. The section along High and Commercial was often referred to as Commercial Row, but was more commonly known as "smoky row." It was a thriving area serving the farming community and canal-generated business of the nineteenth century. A pharmacy, general store and meeting hall brought a steady stream of business. S. B. Dinius operated his harness-making business from the corner of High and Commercial. A wagon maker plied his trade on the west side of the street near where the Richards Bros. hardware store built a weighing station for loads of produce destined for shipping on the railroad. The store also maintained a coal yard and a lumberyard near First Street, where a grist mill operated. It was a tough area, too, as evidenced by three saloons within a stone's throw of each other.

On the Second Street side, buildings stretched down to the canal where warehouses and stables abounded. By 1900, there were groceries and restaurants in the Burdoine building at the corner of Second and Commercial street. The Zent brothers established their first garage along the banks of the McPherren Ditch.

In the 1930s, E. S. and P. A. Thomas established a packing plant at this site, drawing from local farmers for their products. When Thomas Packing Company closed, the town was eager to replace it. A group of merchants including Joseph Merckx was able to convince a new canning company to locate in Roanoke. During the 1940s and early 1950s, residents found seasonal employment at the A. H. Denbo Canning Company, which developed an ingenious process for unloading tomatoes. A load of tomatoes would be weighed on the Richards Bros. scales and then driven to a location on the north side of Second Street, where they would be dumped into a chute that went under Second Street and into the canning factory. This expedited the process of getting the tomatoes into the factory. In a 1946 advertisement Denbo proclaimed it that is was the proud manufacturer of "First Choice Brands and Roanoke Brands Tomato Juice and Quality Tomato Products." It also proudly noted that it was "located in the heart of America's Tomato-Growing Region." That claim would not stand today—90 percent of tomatoes grown in the United States are produced in California.

Robert and Roger Denbo, at left, owned the canning factory that produced Roanoke Brand tomatoes. Indiana ranked first in the nation in acreage devoted to tomatoes for commercial canning from 1929 to 1938 and businesses like this one thrived. The workers were identified in this newspaper photograph as (clockwise from left) Mrs. Joe Miller, Mrs. Alice Gray, Will Hine, Miss Lois Ellis, and Mrs. Allie Dinius.

But High Street also was indicative of problems for the town in its history. A fire, in all likelihood a case of arson, destroyed most of Commercial Row in the 1870s. The main problem was that the town not only lacked fire equipment, but also a fire department. In December 1888, the Masons Hall burned on Commercial Street, taking with it records of the Grand Army of the Republic Post and twenty Civil War muskets. Other businesses burned, including an important stave factory and part of First Street, before the town fathers decided that individuals responding with their buckets weren't enough protection. Through the efforts of residents like Glenn Hartley and George Witherow, the volunteer department either built or bought equipment and became more adept at fighting fires. The first firefighting truck was a Model T that Hartley reconfigured in 1922.

The downtown area of High Street eventually gave rise to homes for workers that did not fare well over the years, especially since they lay in a flood plain between the two small creeks. All were torn down and only one late nineteenth century home remains on First Street near High, and it serves commercial purposes today.

1998

VACANT BUILDING, 102 WEST FIRST STREET
VACANT PROPERTY, 129 NORTH MAIN STREET

HERITAGE CENTER/ZENT COMMONS

On one of the most visible intersections in town sat an empty lot next to a cinder-block building that had been occupied by several businesses that had all failed. These two properties at North Main and West First streets just looked forgotten.

We purchased the building and remodeled it into a permanent home for the Heritage Center. We needed the existing Heritage Center space for the future development of our restaurant, Joseph Decuis. Bob Hoffman, president of the Heritage Center, accepted our recommendation that we move the Heritage Center, for the third time, but in half jest said, "Pete, we appreciate you donating space for the Heritage Center through the years, but we are getting tired of you kicking us out every time you expand. We will move to the new Heritage Center if you allow us to buy it from you once we can generate the necessary funds. We need a permanent home." Bob was as convincing as usual, we were glad to help, and the Heritage Center moved to this location and shortly thereafter purchased the property from us. Bob and the Heritage Center volunteers did a remarkable job in raising the money for the purchase. I think it shows how important preserving Roanoke's heritage is to this small town.

For those envisioning town restoration, the lesson is that the town itself must begin early and continue to demonstrate involvement and financial responsibility for its share of renovation.

The parking lot was converted into a small park. During my business trips to England, I admired small neighborhood parks in London, whose beautiful landscaping and flowers provided a quiet respite to sit and talk to neighbors. We thought that such a park would be a perfect addition to the northwestern corner of Main and First streets.

Once we completed the development of the park, we searched for a name. It didn't take long: the only appropriate name for the park would be Zent Park, named after Bob Zent, the "father of Roanoke history" and the individual who had inspired us to respect Roanoke's heritage when we first moved to town. Bob declined the honor initially, but after thinking it over, he accepted. His efforts at chronicling Roanoke's history will enrich future generations and inspire others to take up the cause.

A public ceremony on May 27, 1999, dedicated Zent Commons. Speakers pointed to the strength of the town's past, present, and future, and a crowd appreciated the new green space.

— Pete Eshelman

★

HISTORY OF MAIN AND FIRST STREETS

In many ways, First and Main is "history corner" for Roanoke. On the site where Zent Commons is now located was one of those ubiquitous storefronts found in small towns. Across First Street, in a somewhat hidden location, is the original town pump whose water refreshed residents and travelers alike outside the Frances Hotel. On the other side of Main Street is the elegant structure that housed the Farmer's State Bank, while diagonally across from

Bob and Kate Hoffman have nurtured the town's collection of historic artifacts and papers for many years.

PETE ESHELMAN'S SPEECH

WE CHOSE to name the commons, Zent Commons, in honor of Robert J. Zent. Bob Zent is a remarkable human being who represents the qualities that make Roanoke so special. His family has been part of our community for 150 years and of his many accomplishments over his almost eighty-nine years, we wish to recognize him for his passion and leadership in preserving the history of this community. His efforts as "Community Historian" have preserved Roanoke's distinctive and colorful tradition. Armed with this proud history, our community leaders are better equipped to make the right decisions for our future.

EXCERPT FROM

ROBERT J. ZENT'S SPEECH

I would like to express the pleasure that my late wife, Kathryn, and I have enjoyed in collecting and sharing our many pictures and news items with different persons and several organizations for publication in our county.

I would like to give credit to Kathryn for her encouragement and her sharing of family photos. Also, to her mother, Mrs. Lydia De Armitt for her contribution of the large collection of Roanoke post cards and many old newspapers.

Also, a great amount of credit is due to my late brother, Kenneth, who meticulously clipped and saved every article that Dr. Koontz wrote for the *Roanoke Review* about his "Civil War Diary" and the "Pioneer Days in Roanoke." He did this when a student at Purdue University during the 1920s. He gave them to me in the 1960s and I in turn had them republished in our local paper.

I appreciate the fact that we have such a nice museum to store and display the many historical items. They have a fine organization and I hope and pray that its presence will be maintained and enjoyed by many future generations.

Robert Zent, 2002

the Commons is the new post office. That site was occupied for many years by a building housing Scott Douglas' furniture store.

Zent Commons was once the site of the Rindchen Building, a structure with two large storefronts that was demolished in the mid-1970s. Its occupants included many men and women who "tried to make a go" of a small restaurant. Some of these endeavors were mildly successful; others were not. Some of the interaction was typical of a small town. One elderly woman remembered being a young girl whose job was to open the Main Café early Sunday morning. She waited on people at the counter and one morning a man came in and asked for bread and milk. She went back to the kitchen where another teenager was working.

"He asked for bread and milk, I told her. How do you make bread and milk?"

"I don't know," the girl said. "I've seen my pa tear it up and drop it in a bowl of milk sometimes. Maybe that's how he wants it."

"So, I decided that was right and carefully broke up the bread and poured milk over it. When I brought it to the counter, the man looked at it for a moment and then at me and said, 'Well, that's the nicest way I've ever been served bread and milk,'" she later reflected. What he may have wanted was simply a slice of bread and a glass of milk.

In addition, the two-story building had a large blank wall on its north side which served as a screen for silent movies sponsored by downtown businessmen in the summers.

Today, a handsome small park leads to the Heritage Center and Museum at the western edge of the commons. In its previous existence, it had been a Laundromat and a bakery. Staffed by local volunteers and financed by private

Volunteers paint a *trompe l'oeil* mural as part of Zent Commons.

donations, the Heritage Center has permanent and changing exhibits illustrating themes from the town's history. The center has coordinated an inventory of eleven local cemeteries, compiling histories, legends and, where possible, a comprehensive listing of grave markers. The inventory was published through contributions of local businesses and the efforts of two dozen Roanoke residents.

The Heritage Center offers written material on the town, including a pamphlet on Roanoke's one-hundred-year-old homes. Researched, written, and prepared by Barbara Behning, the pamphlet includes information on twelve historic homes and a map of their locations. This project, and others like it, will continue through volunteer efforts.

Perhaps the most stunning feature amid the commons flowering shrubs, benches and brick walkways is a large *trompe l'oeil* painted on the wall of the adjoining building on North Main Street. Designed by area artist David Gray and retouched by Peter T. Eshelman, Jr., in 2003, the mural celebrates the heritage of downtown.

★ ★ ★ ★

1999

COLUMBINES, 171 NORTH MAIN STREET, AMBRIOLA'S, 112 NORTH MAIN STREET

171 North Main Street

This building is the only house structure on Main Street between First and Third streets, and we call it The Cottage. The building was owned by Melani Wilson, who had a gift shop named Columbines. Melani is the granddaughter of Mrs. Stabler, who ran Stabler's Drug Store on the corner of Second and Main streets from 1950 to 1965.

We originally asked Melani if we could buy a portion of Columbine's yard. The house had a beautiful side lawn that would work perfectly as a patio for outdoor dining for our building that then was still a corporate dining facility. Melani, who was ready to move on to a new project, suggested we buy the whole building. So we did.

Now part of the Joseph Decuis restaurant complex, The Cottage has been transformed into offices for the restaurant and a private dining room. The side yard, which did provide a beautiful patio for two summers, was changed into a glassed-in conservatory to provide more seating year-round. We bricked in the backyard to create a larger courtyard for al fresco dining.

— *Pete Eshelman*

★

★

112 North Main Street

After fifteen years of building a reputation for great home-style Italian food, Denny Ambriole made the decision to change careers and sold his restaurant on contract. Within a short period of time, the restaurant went out of business and Denny repossessed the business and property. Denny contacted me and asked if we were interested in the building and his business. Our company's private corporate dining room had become very successful, and we were toying with the idea of expanding it into a gourmet restaurant open to the public. Our chef, Lisa Williams, had wowed our clients for several years with excellent gourmet food and she was ready for the challenge. But we were lacking a liquor license, which would be a necessity for a gourmet restaurant. Denny owned one of the few liquor licenses available in town, and we were informed no new liquor licenses would be issued in the near future. We bought Denny's business, building, and liquor license.

We gutted the building and to our surprise found a most beautiful and original tin ceiling, which we restored. Our corporate photographer, Steve Vorderman, was interested in moving his business from Fort Wayne to Roanoke and opening up an art gallery, and we remodeled the space to accommodate Steve's needs as a photography studio and art gallery.

— *Pete Eshelman*

★

the studio and gallery of a professional photographer. The building's large windows and high, decorative ceilings make it an ideal location for an exhibition of artwork.

There is more to the history of this building than meets the eye. Prior to the current structure, there was a two-story frame building that once housed F.G. Chenneour's drugstore and later a business operated by Preston B. Settlemyre, president of the Roanoke Drain Tile Company, and his son-in-law, Nathan Highlands. Settlemyre sold the property to the bank in June 1916 and the building was razed before the U.S. entry into World War I. Across the top of the current structure is engraved "Farmer's State Bank," reflecting its earliest manifestation. The bank was organized in 1915 by a D. L. Zinstmaster, a Huntington man who specialized in such startups. Settlemyre served as the bank's president into the early 1920s. He died in 1932 after nine years' illness.

Advertising itself as "The Bank That Backs the Farmer," it was smaller than its competitor at the opposite end of the North Main Street block. But both banks were competitive. A November 1920 issue of the *Roanoke Review* announced that both banks would now be open from 7 to 9 P.M. on Saturdays rather than Wednesdays, aiming to better serve the busy town on Saturday evenings. Business was good during this period, and Settlemyre described 1920–1921 as "largest in history" for the bank.

Both banks had front-page advertisements on September 1, 1923, concerning their respective balance sheets. Farmer's was smaller and furthermore its cash on hand seemed precariously small: $4,328; while First National's cash on hand was reported at $36,513.

That winter tragedy struck the Farmer's State Bank operation. The president of the bank was G. I. Shank, who on the morning of December 20, 1923, went for a drive with his daughter in a brand new Ford coupe. The morning was reportedly foggy, and whether Shank didn't see the oncoming interurban or whether he tried to outrace it in his new car, the result was a ghastly accident that killed both occupants of the car. The impact tore off the streetcar's brakes and it continued down the tracks for a quarter mile after the impact. Shank was sixty-two years old.

In two months, the Farmer's State Bank was apparently in financial trouble. In February 1924, it merged with the First National Bank and they became First & Farmers State Bank with capital of forty thousand dollars. All of the operations were moved to First National by March 1. Farmers remained an important consumer element, though. On February 29, 1924, the combined bank advertised that "75 percent of all accounts and transactions are with farmers."

The building at 112 North Main remained the property of the combined financial institutions until 1935 when, in the liquidation of the failed First & Farmers, it was sold to Scott J. Douglas. It was used as a warehouse for his furniture store across First Street for more than twenty years. Douglas, who came to Roanoke in 1900 as a cabinet maker for Wasmuth Company, operated Douglas Furniture Store from 1910 to the 1950s. He was known for having an excellent selection of period furniture, attracting customers throughout the region. There was some irony in Douglas' using the former bank for storage. Douglas was known in town for not trusting banks and refusing to keep his money in them. One local legend tells of Douglas selling a large sofa to a couple in Fort Wayne and, after it was delivered, remembering that he had secreted some cash beneath its cushions when it sat in his store. He reputedly drove to the buyers' home and gained entrance by telling them he wanted to be certain of the sofa's quality. He sat down on it, carefully inserted his hands beneath the cushions and, unbeknownst to the couple, retrieved an envelope with six thousand dollars in cash that he had placed there.

After Douglas' death in the summer of 1957, the building was leased by Cecil Rittenour, who opened the Tall Pines Café in February 1958. Serving breakfast and noon dinners, the restaurant seated forty. With its fountain service and juke box, the Tall Pines was "the place to go to" after a basketball game at Roanoke High School for burgers and Cokes in the 1960s. It also was known for Norma Rittenour's pies, and Steve Williams remembers that salesmen's visits to the Roanoke Hardware Store "often seemed to somehow coincide with Norma's pies coming out of the oven."

Norman and Sue Brown bought the property in April 1974 from the estate of Douglas's widow, Della, and in subsequent years the building housed Z Place, which was a pizza restaurant, and Ambriola's.

★ ★ ★ ★

2000

ICE CREAM PARLOR, 139 NORTH MAIN STREET

The second ice cream shop at this location in five years closed down, regretfully, because every town needs a quality ice cream shop. Many people have fond memories of walking downtown on summer nights and enjoying ice cream cones there. It is a great family activity, part of small-town atmosphere at its best.

American Specialty purchased this building. The exterior has been remodeled in a Victorian theme. Alice tells me ice cream will be returning to downtown Roanoke.

Small-town revitalization efforts need to include several walking family destinations: unique boutiques and ice cream or candy shops are good examples.

— *Pete Eshelman*

HISTORY OF 139 NORTH MAIN STREET

There were two two-story buildings on this parcel at one time. The southerly building was divided in half. The most southerly part contained the Double Dip owned by Joe Leaper. The other side held the Main Street Café when it was owned by the Crows and before that by Benjamin Blum.

The other building, where Rex's Barber Shop is now located, contained the Sandwich Inn, operated by Dale Rollins. Prior to that it was a restaurant run by Urban Henry. In 1933, though, the Sandwich Inn was the subject of some controversy. The *Roanoke Review* carried a small, almost unnoticeable headline on page 1 on July 14: "Beer Placed on Sale Here." That the Sandwich Inn ended twenty-seven years of Roanoke being "dry" was perhaps less important than the term it engendered. As other eating establishments in the vicinity gained licenses to sell liquor over the years, many of the young people found themselves excluded, causing them to refer to the establishment as "beer joints." It was an appellation, some say today, that fails to do justice to the good home-cooked food at the Sandwich Inn and its successors in town.

The former Betty's Ice Cream parlor was acquired by American Specialty in June 2000 and handsomely renovated in the spring of 2003.

JOSEPH DECUIS, 191 NORTH MAIN STREET

In today's world, a great restaurant can put a small town on the map. It's like owning a major-league sports team in a big city. Roanoke has had many fine restaurants over the years, attracting a loyal clientele. For example, Roanoke's Village Inn has been an important part of the town's Main Street for fifty years.

In 2000 we opened Joseph Decuis, a gourmet dining restaurant, to the public. The restaurant was named after my ancestor who lived in Louisiana from 1750 to 1820 and began our heritage of dining in the Creole tradition. The Creoles believed that proper dining was important to quality of life. Alice and I believe that in today's fast-food, fast-paced world, proper dining and gourmet food are important pleasures of life not to be lost. So with Lisa Williams' talent for great food and our own love of great food, we opened Joseph Decuis.

Many people thought a gourmet restaurant in Roanoke would never succeed. We heard comments like "a high-end restaurant in small town like Roanoke will never make it" and "Roanoke is too far away from any cities to make it work."

Following the crowd has never been our forte. We believed that the quality of food prepared by our executive chef and staff was outstanding and other people would love it, too. We had confidence that Joseph Decuis would become a destination restaurant: its small-town location and New Orleans-style atmosphere would provide a completely different experience from that of the typical restaurant locations in shopping centers and strip malls of the surrounding area. We also believed that the Fort Wayne area needed a world-class restaurant.

Alice became proprietor, and Alice and Lisa worked as a team in turning our corporate dining facility into a public enterprise. Today, the restaurant complex includes half of the western side of North Main Street: three connected buildings, four distinct dining rooms, and a courtyard for al fresco dining. It has earned a reputation as the finest restaurant in the area and a destination for out of town travelers. Of everything we have done in Roanoke, Joseph Decuis has done the most to put Roanoke on the map.

Not every small town rebuilding itself may be able to create a Joseph Decuis, but building or attracting a renowned gourmet restaurant will pay great dividends in bringing new people to town and developing a national identity.

— *Pete Eshelman*

Joseph Decuis is an award-winning gourmet restaurant that has gained renown for its wine dinners. Tables are arranged lavishly for the Renaissance Dinner (left), which has become a popular annual event.

2001

COLLINS PROPERTY, 146 SOUTH MAIN STREET
NELSON'S, 314 NORTH MAIN

The year 2001 was looking like another great year of growth for American Specialty. Then the tragedy of September 11 occurred. Like the rest of the world, our clients were profoundly affected. The insurance industry was thrown into turmoil, and suddenly insuring sports and entertainment became a life-and-death business. On September 12 we redirected our resources and within weeks developed new risk services desperately needed by our clients. Our clients needed us and we responded.

Our employees were traumatized, too. We held meetings to discuss the tragedy and ways to respond positively. In an effort to boost morale, we did the "obvious thing": We purchased a golden retriever puppy. Camille came to the office with me every day and greeted the employees first thing in the morning. She had an incredible effect on boosting employee morale and earned the distinguished title of "CMO"— Chief Morale Officer. Sometimes difficult times require creative solutions.

We purchased two new properties to address our continual need for parking and to accommodate anticipated future growth.

146 SOUTH MAIN STREET

The Collins property came up for sale and we purchased the property and converted it to desperately needed parking for our growing business. By 2001, our businesses employed 128 employees who all drove to work and needed space for their cars.

314 NORTH MAIN STREET

This building includes thirty-six thousand square feet and became vacant after Steve Cadwallader moved his manufacturing business to Huntington in a new facility. Steve was very involved in community organizations and loved Roanoke, but needed a more modern, more easily accessible plant for his growing fabricating business. We purchased the building and currently use it as a maintenance and storage facility with future plans for office and retail development.

— *Pete Eshelman*

HISTORY OF 314 NORTH MAIN STREET

In its early years, this building was part of the Wasmuth complex of buildings serving the community. The A. Wasmuth Hardware Store operated at the north end of the family lumberyard, just across Third Street. Next door was a frame structure, now demolished, that carried some of the finest building supplies in the region. Many fine homes were built in the area using lumber and materials from Wasmuth's.

It was in April 1936, a particularly difficult point in the Great Depression, that the Roanoke newspaper proudly reported the Roanoke Businessmen's Association had met with the owners of Fort Wayne Coils and convinced them to establish a manufacturing operation in the old Wasmuth Hardware Building. Within weeks, the new company was advertising for experienced coil winders and finishers. Within two years, the factory was operating at capacity, making electrical coils for ignitions and motors that would soon prove vital to America's manufacturing of war materiel.

The founder of the Coil Engineering and Manufacturing Company, as the business was renamed when the relocation to Roanoke was completed, was Eugene Strait, an engineer born in Muncie in 1904. In addition to the Roanoke business, he founded Wabash Magnetics and All-Coil. He was an entrepreneurial engineer and his companies prospered during World War II. The Coil Engineering and Manufacturing became the town's largest manufacturer, employing more than four hundred people during the peak production period in the war. The importance of its work was evident when the War Department ordered the town to close a portion of Third Street and

Above: Wasmuth's hardware and agricultural implements store at North Main and Third streets. At the left is building since razed that carried Wasmuth's homebuilding supplies.

Right: Coil winders (from left) Richard Augspurger, Miss Marcene McCaughey, and Robert Hine are shown in this September 21, 1946, newspaper photograph.

an alley access way, and place fences around the factory to ensure security at the plant.

As with the rest of the nation, the war brought unprecedented employment opportunities for women in the Roanoke area, notably at the Coil plant. Women and high school students made up the bulk of the workers, with men hired for supervision and wrapping of the heavier coils.

After the war, the entire interests of the company were purchased by Clifford A. McBride of Providence, Rhode Island, who owned and operated plastic, chemical and other plants. But no change in on-site management was made, and the company continued to operate, although the pace of the war years' production abated.

In 1966 operating as the Square D Coil Factory, the company honored Mrs. Lenore Richards, Elwood Jennings, and Jacob Merckx for their quarter-century of service at the factory. The event was among Coil's final activities, as the company ceased operations in 1967, and the building was purchased by Paul Hunckler of Huntington for a new company called Pick-A-Nut. It produced handy packets of metal fasteners for builders.

In 1986 Nelson Machining and Fabricating moved into the former Coil Factory building. Founded by Steve Cadwallader, Nelson fabricated, machined, and welded custom metal assemblies for industry. Nelson moved to larger facilities in nearby Huntington in 2000.

The lone reminder of the Coil Factory's operation is its chimney, which still can be seen from Main Street. The building was acquired in September 2001 and is being renovated as part of the American Specialty corporate campus.

2002

C&M PROPERTIES, SOUTH MAIN AND VINE STREETS
E. J. RICHARDS' HOUSE, 492 NORTH MAIN STREET

The year 2002 started with an enormous challenge as we were responsible for specialized insurance and risk-management services for the Salt Lake City Winter Olympic Games, the second Olympics on U.S. soil in a decade. We became the only risk-management company with the enviable distinction of providing those services for the two historic events. In response to the heightened threat of terrorism caused by the September 11 attacks, security was the overwhelming factor in the entire risk-management program, and we were well prepared. Several of our employees worked on-site at the Games, and as a company, we took great pride in contributing to the Games' success.

Our business has doubled in four years, and we ended 2002 with another significant milestone. We won the contract to provide insurance, claims management, and risk-management services for all the clubs in Major League baseball. From our perspective, this was the crown jewel in professional sports. This proved to our employees what Dave, Tim, and I believe so strongly: that patience and persistence pay. Furthermore, Joseph Decuis had earned the reputation as the finest dining experience in northeast Indiana. We have grown to 146 employees and added two more properties to our Roanoke corporate campus.

C&M PROPERTIES, SOUTH MAIN AND VINE STREETS

We purchased two C&M properties from REDO. The small property will be landscaped into a greenbelt providing an attractive entrance into town. The second parcel of land will be developed into future parking to accommodate over ninety cars. This parking will be used for American Specialty's growth and the town's future parking needs.

— *Pete Eshelman*

★

HISTORY OF SOUTH MAIN AND VINE STREETS

The site of Roanoke's environmental calamity was once a Miami camp-ground—almost into the twentieth century. A celebration for Kilsoquah brought many Native Americans to the town, for the festivities and news-paper articles from the time indicate they set up camp at Main and Vine. It was apparently a spot of longtime use by the Miami because elderly men tell of finding arrowheads and pottery fragments at the site when they were boys.

The first major construction of note was when Ed and Homer Couture erected a building on the southwest corner that eventually housed their service station. In the 1920s, it also served as a showroom for the local dealership Willys and Knight automobiles. Another garage was built across Vine Street near where M. L. Dague's flouring mill was powered by Cow Creek since the early days of the town. This garage eventually became the waste-water treatment facility for the ill-fated factory across the street.

Continental Plating purchased the Couture building after World War II and began its operations. From a small company, the electroplating operation grew into the town's largest employer in thirty-five years. The world of C&M Plating changed as the entire country became aware of the nation's growing environmental hazards and new laws were promulgated to stop pollution and punish polluters. The old methods of storing and disposing chemical wastes were banned and the new environmental agencies cracked down on violators. This occurred throughout the nation, although the Midwest, with its history of heavy manufacturing, found itself significantly affected. The burden for cleanup was especially difficult for small towns like Roanoke that lacked the personnel to recognize and mitigate environmental hazards. In addition, the small towns found themselves unable to afford hazardous-waste cleanups because of their small tax base. All of these factors contributed to Roanoke's "environmental nightmare," as the *Herald-Press* referred to it. The town was the focus of considerable media attention as the scale of the environmental problems became known. Then, on July 28, 1988, the leak of a corrosive liquid caused the evacuation of about two hundred people from their homes. It put Roanoke into national headlines that the town's leaders did not want.

The buildings sat empty for eight years before Huntington County condemned them and ordered their demolition. In October 1995 and March 1996, several construction companies razed the buildings. Interestingly, it was completed as a volunteer effort, demonstrating how a small town works together to solve its problems.

492 North Main Street

This home is one of the finest representations of Victorian architecture in Roanoke. E. J. Richards methodically restored the home to preserve its historic character, and when his mother died, he moved into her home on Third Street and restored it with

The elegant charm of the Victorian architecture of E. J. Richards' home has been restored for the Inn at Joseph Decuis.

the same care. Prior to putting his 492 North Main Street home on the market, he contacted me to ask if American Specialty would be interested in purchasing the home. Anyone driving by the home would have recognized its special charm. We purchased the home and have converted it to the Inn at Joseph Decuis to provide accommodations for out-of-town guests who visit the restaurant.

— Pete Eshelman

★

HISTORY OF 492 NORTH MAIN STREET

As Main Street rises toward the north and passes a variety of homes from different periods of the town's history, a stately white house with a broad porch occupies the southeast corner at Fifth Street. It is a beautiful example of home construction of its period and carries a history in itself. Believed to be a Sears "Four Square" catalogue home, the structure was built in 1912 for the Wasmuth family. It sits on one of the lots of the Chapman and Horton addition that became part of the town in 1846. The first home was built in the 1860s, and among its owners was pharmacist Charles L. Hackett. The Wasmuths acquired it in 1896 and built the current structure sixteen years later, drawing materials from their lumber mill. As a result, the woodwork and workmanship is among the finest of its time.

Eventually, the home was transferred to Daniel A. Wasmuth after the death of his father, Augustus. The president of the First & Farmer's bank, Wasmuth lived there until the early 1930s when the Great Depression forced his bank into insolvency and him into personal bankruptcy. Eugene Strait, the owner of the Coil Manufacturing and Engineering Company, and his wife Cecile bought it for the appraised value of two thousand dollars in July 1938. It remained in the Strait family until it was sold to Bob Bear and then to E. J. Richards in 1990.

In 2002 it was purchased for the creation of a bed and breakfast.

★

AFTERWORD

THIRTEEN YEARS LATER

Thirteen years after moving to Roanoke I again look out my window from the second floor of my office. I see mature, lush Bradford Pear trees glistening in the sunshine along Main Street. The brick-lined sidewalks are dressed up with potted flowers in front of each building. Baskets blooming with red flowers hang from the antique streetlights. The building facades are inviting, with their restored turn-of-the-century charm, each with its own personality. A teacher walks by with her second grade class from the Roanoke Elementary School. Anyone who has walked with twenty-five seven year olds knows it's an exercise in "herding cats," but the teacher has solved the challenge of managing energetic, inquisitive children by having them hold on to a rope. The air is filled with their chatter and laughter. The teacher stops the caravan and tells the children to notice the beautiful flowers on Main Street, but please don't pick them. Of course, a little boy in the back picks a flower. He hands it to the little girl holding the rope beside him. I won't tell. I hope that little boy and girl are enriched by picking that flower. Watching them, I am.

I think about our business and how far we have come. Thirteen years ago, we started at 142 North Main Street with six employees. We have grown to more than 150 great people.

I am proud of American Specialty. In our unassuming little town, we have grown to become an important business serving an important industry. Insurance is a noble business. In fact, it is the foundation for the world's economies; without insurance, no one could take risk, innovate, or grow. It is also one of the most complicated financial instruments in the world, which makes it ever challenging. The industry we serve, the Sports/Entertainment industry, is an important industry. On the surface, it appears to be glitz and glitter, but its purpose is much deeper. It provides the platform for the development of a peaceful global community. It sets the stage for humankind to compete under one set of rules, proving that people from diverse cultures can live peacefully together. The role we play today as a leader in providing insurance and risk management services for this industry is significant and important. We understand our responsibility and accept it with great respect. Yes, we have come a long way proving that my dad was right. "Success is luck, the harder you work, the luckier you get." Striving for the American dream is a good thing.

★

The Future

What does the future hold? By definition the future cannot be controlled. But I come from the school that taught: if you develop a plan and believe in it, you can influence the future.

Here is the plan I believe in. We will continue to grow our insurance and risk consulting business serving the Sports/Entertainment industry. As this industry grows, we will help it grow. This will require a unique discipline, "seeing the world for what it really is and not for what one hopes it to be." Risk management is a business for thinkers.

Our small town of Roanoke will be challenged in a world where small town problems are unlikely to appear on the radar screens of big business and the federal government. Count on it! But unlike the insurance business, success will require envisioning Roanoke for what "one hopes it to be." Our success will attract likeminded businesses to Roanoke. I hope our success inspires likeminded businesses to move to small towns seeking revival across America.

Joseph Decuis, our superstar retail business, will attract new retail businesses, and the downtown will become a center for quality family entertainment events.

Roanoke's renewed small town quality of life will attract new people to town, people who will restore old homes.

In the next decade or sooner, Roanoke must permanently solve its greatest threat: flooding. A catastrophic flood would turn Roanoke into a footnote in history. If Walt Disney was able to figure out how to drain a swamp in central Florida to become the home of Disney World, we can solve Roanoke's flooding problem. This will require developing a strategic plan and getting on the radar screen of county, state and federal government agencies that must assist.

Long range, strategic planning must happen. This type of planning doesn't normally happen in small towns. Planning is a huge issue; the sweat behind any success. I predict that in the next thirteen years, small towns that do not plan for their futures for such things as managing growth, infrastructure needs, and fiscal responsibility will become footnotes in history. Either you plan for your community's future, or risk someone else planning it for you. Why take the chance?

★

A Defining Moment

All of our lives have defining moments: your first home run, your wedding, the birth of your children, the death of a loved one.

On September 11, 2001, my adult life changed as I watched CNN live on the television in my office and observed the blatant murder of innocent people while enemies used civilian airplanes against us as lethal weapons. By the end of that day, my grief for the victims and shock knowing our way of life was under attack turned into a new sense of purpose. I knew that it was time for me to live for others: my family, my business, community and country. God willing, they will be here long after me. We are temporary residents on this planet, and the mark we leave is the good we can bring, no matter how small or grand. In fact, I have learned that a hundred small good deeds are most of the time better than one big one. In life, consistent base hits are more important than a home run.

When I think about this, my mind shifts to Zent Commons, where a time capsule was buried in 2000 and will be opened in 2050. I envision myself standing there at ninety-eight years of age, waiting for someone to open the capsule and comment, "American Specialty was a good company and did a great job in helping Roanoke be a better place." I hope our example inspires others.

★

Thanks, Rex

One of my great pleasures in Roanoke is getting my haircut at Rex's Barber Shop. His barbershop is located across from our office on Main Street. He has two barber chairs, yet he only uses one, as he is the only barber. There is no need for a director of human resources.

The barbershop evokes fond memories of my thirteen years in Roanoke. While sitting in Rex's barber chair, I see the checkerboard that sits on the top of a wooden table with two high back chairs. As I reminisce, I see a blond-haired, blue-eyed, happy five-year-old boy and his dad playing checkers, waiting for haircuts: my son, Peter, and me. Peter always won. A dad, his boy, and haircuts are special. It's a dad thing.

While waiting for my turn in Rex's chair, I like watching dads, moms, sons, and daughters playing checkers while waiting for their haircuts. I know what they are feeling.

I like looking into the picture directly in front of the barber chair hanging on the wood paneled wall, located in a position where you are obliged to study it. I know Rex purposely placed it there. After years of haircuts, it has etched an indelible impression in my mind, and I'm sure in the minds of all customers who have sat in Rex's barber chair. It is a painting of two blacksmiths at work. One blacksmith is laboring over an anvil by a hot coal fire. If you use your imagination, you can feel the blacksmith's sweat roll off his face and sense his determination to create the perfect horseshoe. You can hear the indistinguishable sound of his hammer striking hot iron. An old workhorse is standing peacefully being shod by the other blacksmith. The horse stands free, its reins hanging to the ground. It knows the routine. It has been there before. It is a perfect summer day, blue skies above treetops, and a young barefooted boy stands by watching. You wonder what he is thinking. Perhaps his dad is the blacksmith making the horseshoe, and he is hoping that his father will teach him the trade. The painting is soothing, and it prompts thinking about what's important in life.

Sitting in Rex's chair is a transcendental experience. Rex has been in business as a barber for forty-three years, forty-one of these years in Roanoke. When I ask, he will tell me his philosophy on running a business, creating value for customers, pricing his product, and managing the bottom line in good and bad economic times. I find the fundamental elements of success in his business are lessons for my business or any business. One day I told Mike Perkins, the editor of the *Huntington Herald-Press*, that sitting in Rex's chair is like listening to Warren Buffet at his annual convention. Rex's observations and advice on business and life should be a column in his newspaper and *The Wall Street Journal.*

In between our conversations, I look out Rex's front window facing Main Street and see a beautiful tree, planted eleven years ago during the beautification project. At that time, Rex asked us to adjust the planting of the tree by two feet to the left so it would grow squarely in the middle of his storefront window. The tree has matured, and his foresight in recommending where it was planted has enhanced his view and the view his customers see on Main Street. No doubt he gave a lot of thought to the position of planting that tree; another great business lesson, vision.

As I sit in his barber chair, beyond the tree I see a beautiful Main Street. This gives me a feeling of great pride and accomplishment. I cannot help but think that others feel the same way as they look out Rex's window.

What do I look forward to? I look forward to each day's challenges. Personally, I like problem solving, fighting battles, accomplishing things other people say "can't be done" and creating opportunity for people to grow. I look forward to completing our projects in Roanoke that are on the drawing board and, I look forward to hearing of success stories of village restorations like ours, to the renewed hope restoration brings to those whose hopes may have faltered; and to the great benefits that strong small towns will bring to America's future.

Finally, I especially look forward to my next haircut at Rex's Barber Shop.

Two prominent contributors to the quality of life in today's Roanoke: barber Rex Ottinger and retired engineer Leon Burrey.

1990

1990 American Specialty purchases first building in Roanoke for its business.

1992 Roanoke Beautification Committee formed—American Specialty leads a volunteer effort to improve Roanoke's historic downtown.

1993 Downtown Beautification Project completed. Business owners, volunteers, and elected officials work together using private dollars to fund the improvements.

Roanoke Heritage Center and Museum is established.

American Specialty purchases 199 North Main Street to become future home of Heritage Center.

1994 American Specialty purchases 156 North Main Street for office expansion.

American Specialty purchases land on 267 East First Street and demolishes derelict home and converts to parking.

1995

1995 A group of citizens form the Roanoke Economic Development Organization (REDO) and successfully acquire the C&M Plating property and work with governmental officials to eliminate environmental hazard.

American Specialty purchases 141 North Main Street, preserving the home of the Rebekah's Lodge, and converts second floor into corporate fitness center.

1996 Roanoke Beautification Foundation is established to provide a permanent means to maintain Roanoke's beautification heritage for future generations.

American Specialty acquires to-be-condemned home on 208 Vine Street and converts property to greenbelt.

196 North Main Street purchased by American Specialty for corporate offices and guest suites.

Company purchases 164 North Main Street for office expansion.

Beautification Committee starts tradition of hanging flower baskets on Main Street lampposts.

1996

1996 American Specialty purchases 191 North Main Street and moves Heritage Center into this new location.

Corporate dining facility in the former Roanoke State Bank opened by American Specialty.

1997 Vacant lot on property on High Streets purchased and improved for expanded parking.

1997 On July 3, Roanoke's Patriotic Pops Concert is inaugurated on Main Street, becoming the region's premier family entertainment event.

1998 American Specialty purchases empty lot on the corner of Main and First streets that becomes a community park named Zent Commons in honor of Robert Zent, the "father" of Roanoke history, and a vacant building on an adjoining parcel on First Street that becomes the permanent home of the Heritage Center and Museum.

1999 Property at 171 North Main Street is purchased by American Specialty and becomes part of the Joseph Decuis restaurant facility.

American Specialty purchases 112 North Main Street, which becomes a photography studio and art gallery.

2000

2000 Building at 139 North Main Street is purchased by American Specialty, with the goal of remodeling it for future retail space.

Roanoke's Town Court expands and remodels in the beautification theme.

American Specialty expands its corporate dining facility and establishes Joseph Decuis, a gourmet dining restaurant which gains national acclaim.

2001 American Specialty purchases 146 South Main Street, which is converted into additional parking.

Former factory at 314 North Main Street is obtained by American Specialty for future office and retail expansion.

2002 American Specialty purchases 492 North Main Street and converts this historic home into the Inn at Joseph Decuis.

American Specialty purchases the remaining C&M Plating property from REDO which will be developed into additional downtown parking.

Acknowledgments

ROANOKE HAS become a very special part of our corporate life, a labor of love, and we have been fortunate to have worked with many great people in the community who have mentored us, encouraged us, inspired us, worked with us, and cried and laughed with us as we have developed our businesses and participated in Roanoke's revival. We would like to specially recognize the following individuals:

Alice, Peter, Jr., Eliza, and Hilary Eshelman, American Specialty employees and clients, Bob and Kate Hoffman, Bob Humphries, Bob and Nancy Kelsey, Bob Rose, Bob Sunday, Bob and Kolleen Turpin, Bob Zent, Col. Perry Collins, Dad and Mom, Dale Carroll and family, Dale, Virginia, and Gary Fry, Dave Harris, DeLoss Hartley, Dick Smart, E. J. Richards, Ed Coy, Elsie Wygant, Eugene Parker, Mr. Harold Amstutz, John Klingenberger, John Mathe, John and Linda Pulver, Kay and Patty Ratcliff, Kevin Quickery, Kevin Yoder, Leon Burrey, Marilyn Hoy, Monk Ward, Melanie Reukauf, Mr. Joe Merckx, Mr. Ralph Hine, Paul Roth, Paul Swain and crew, Rex Ottinger, Rich and Karen Pape, Steve and Michelle Schwieterman, Terri Taylor, Tim, Wally Orr, and William Wren.

Also, Dr. Ann McPherren, Amanda Allen, B. Joan Keefer, Barbara W. Bushnell, Prof. Bruce Bigelow of Butler University, Dale Scott, Dan Weir, Daryl Schrock, David Gray, Harmon Murbach, J. C. Creager Smith, Marjorie Przeracki, Michael Hawfield, Mike Perkins, Mike Rogers, Nancy Baxter, Norman A. Richards, Pam Gray, Patricia Kelsey Watkins, Patti Fritz, Phyllis Witherow, Randy Rowe, Rose Meldrum, Steve Vorderman, Steve Williams, Thomas Castaldi, Thomas McPherren, Velma Runyon, and William McPherren.

BIBLIOGRAPHY

Atherton, Lewis. *Main Street on the Middle Border.* Bloomington: Indiana University Press, 1954.

Bash, Frank Sumner, ed. *History of Huntington County.* 2 vols. Chicago: Lewis Publishing Company, 1914.

Cayton, Andrew R. L. and Susan E. Gray, eds. *The American Midwest: Essays on Regional History.* Bloomington: Indiana University Press, 2001.

Cole, Charlie. *The Soil & Soul Connection.* Kearney, Nebraska: Morris Publishing, 2001.

Danbom, David B. *Born in the Country: A History of Rural America.* Baltimore: The Johns Hopkins University Press, 1995.

Frankcaviglia, Richard V. *Main Street Revisited: Time, Space, and Image Building in Small-Town America.* Iowa City: University of Iowa Press, 1996.

———. *History of Huntington County.* Chicago: Brant & Fuller, 1887.

Indiana Historic Sites and Structures Inventory. *Huntington County, Interim Report, 2nd Edition.* March 1997.

Kinietz, W. Vernon. *The Indians of the Western Great Lakes, 1615–1760.* Ann Arbor: University of Michigan Press, 1940.

Koontz, Dr. S. *Pioneer Days in Roanoke Canal Days.* Privately printed, 1961.

Mahoney, Timothy R. *River Towns in the Great West: The Structure of Provincial Urbanization in the American Midwest, 1820–1870.* New York: Cambridge University Press, 1990.

Martindale, Don and R. Galen Hanson. *Small Town and the Nation.* Westport, Conn.: Greenwood Publishing, 1969.

Phillips, Clifton J. *Indiana In Transition: The Emergence of an Industrial Commonwealth, 1880–1920.* Indianapolis: Indiana Historical Bureau & Indiana Historical Society, 1968.

Poinsatte, Charles R. *Fort Wayne During the Canal Era, 1828–1855.* Indianapolis: Indiana Historical Bureau, 1969.

Potterf, Rex M. *Little River Drainage Project.* Fort Wayne, Ind.: Allen County-Fort Wayne Historical Society, 1968.

Raffert, Stewart. *The Miami Indians of Indiana: A Persistent People, 1654–1994.* Indianapolis: Indiana Historical Society, 1996.

Roll, Charles. *Indiana: One Hundred and Fifty Years of American Development.* 5 vols. Chicago: Lewis Publishing Company, 1931.

Vidich, Arthur J. and Joseph Bensman. *Small Town in Mass Society: Class, Power, and Religion in a Rural Community.* Princeton, N.J.: Princeton University Press, 1958.

Wasmuth, E. M. *The Saga of a Hoosier Village.* Privately printed, 1999.

Young, Frank W. *Small Towns in Multilevel Society.* Lanham, Md.: University Press of America, 1999.

NEWSPAPERS

Evening Herald (Huntington, Indiana)

Fort Wayne News-Sentinel

Four Corners Courier (Roanoke, Indiana)

Huntington Democrat

Huntington Herald

Huntington Herald-Press

Huntington Press

Huntington Weekly Herald

The Morning Times (Huntington, Indiana)

Roanoke Dispatch

The Roanoke Review

Roanoke Weekly Post

DIRECTORIES

Polk Directories. Huntington County, Indiana: Including Towns of Andrews, Bippus, Buckeye, Lancaster, Majenica, Markle, Mount Etna, Roanoke, and Warren, also Huntington County Taxpayers. Detroit, Michigan: Polk Directories, 1920–1932.

Huntington City Directory and *Huntington County Gazeteer*, 1911–1912. Anderson, Indiana: Union Directory Company.

PHOTOGRAPHY CREDITS

MAIN TEXT:

Roanoke Area Heritage Center, pages 7, 12, 14, 21, 25, 26, 28, 30, 70, 74, 77, 79 and 99; Bob Rose (illustrations), pages ii, 16 and 22; E. J. Richards, pages 14, 29, 33 and 82; Norman A. Richards, pages 26, 29 and 57; the Fairchild family, page 19; Bill McPherren, pages 14 and 41; John Klingenberger, pages 45 and 47; the Zent Collection, pages 16, 22, 28, 33, 39 and 81; Steve Vorderman, pages xiii, 42, 43, 50, 89, 90, 97, 102, 107 and 110; Tim Eshelman, page 91; Shirley Harris, page 61; Guild Press Emmis Books, pages 2, 5, 6 (illustrated by Richard Day) and 10 (illustrated by Steven D. Armour); Ronald May, page 65; and from "Rotogravure" of the *Fort Wayne News-Sentinel* (September 21, 1946), pages 87 and 99.

COLOR INSERT:

Contemporary photograph of Farmers State Bank by Tim Eshelman. All other contemporary photographs by Steve Vorderman; 1980s photographs by Bob Turpin; all Patriotic Pops photos by Shirley Harris.